TONY GARNIER:
THE CITÉ INDUSTRIELLE

PLANNING AND CITIES

PLANNING AND CITIES

General Editor

GEORGE R. COLLINS, Columbia University

TONY GARNIER:
THE CITÉ INDUSTRIELLE

DORA WIEBENSON

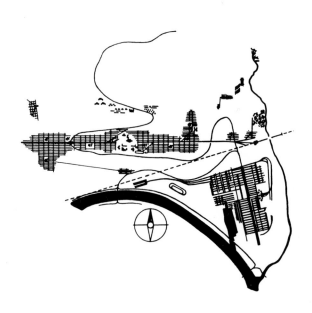

GEORGE BRAZILLER   NEW YORK

CONTENTS

GENERAL EDITOR'S PREFACE

The purpose of the present series of books on cities and planning is to make available to those who are concerned about current urban problems some information about the ways in which cities have formed or have been theoretically conceived in various historical periods and cultural areas. No period is more vital to our interests than the immediate past. Since about 1900 a number of architects have produced special images of the modern city that have considerably influenced the popular idea of the urban environment.

Tony Garnier is a case in point. By the time that our modern architecture had matured in the 1920's, many characteristics of Garnier's ideal city-for-industry had become dogma to the progressists: zoning for usage, specialized centers, insulating greenery, simplified architectural masses, modern clean power, and concrete construction. Dora Wiebenson describes the cultural setting in which Garnier developed his Cité Industrielle and suggests to us how the Cité summed up many utopian and technological aspirations of city planners of the late nineteenth and early twentieth centuries.

It is our hope that a series of concise, illustrated volumes on individual planners like Garnier will, with our books about different epochs and areas, provide a complement to the longer survey books that deal with architectural city planning and urban history in general.

G.R.C.

PREFACE

One of the more important but enigmatic figures of the modern planning movement is Tony Garnier (1869–1948). Little is known about his life, or about the influences on him which led to his creation of the project on which his fame now rests, the Cité Industrielle. Only in a recent work by Christophe Pawlowski, *Tony Garnier et les débuts de l'urbanisme fonctionelle en France* (Paris, 1967), do the known pertinent facts about Garnier seem to be discussed in any detail. Because this work, as, indeed, most literature on Garnier, stresses the contribution of the Cité to later twentieth-century city planning, it is the purpose of our book to discuss Garnier's work as a product of its particular environment, and to investigate its place as a bridge both between nineteenth- and twentieth-century planning theory and between academic and nonacademic architectural theories and techniques.

Sections of the following discussion are based on my article, "Utopian Aspects of Tony Garnier's Cité Industrielle," which appeared in the March, 1960, issue of the *Journal of the Society of Architectural Historians*. I am indebted to M. Louis Weckerlin, *architecte-en-chef* of Lyons, who many years ago generously shared with me his wealth of knowledge about Garnier's work and attitudes. I would also like to thank George R. Collins of Columbia University, who from time to time has encouraged me in my interest in Tony Garnier.

D. W.

INTRODUCTION:
DESCRIPTION OF
THE CITÉ INDUSTRIELLE

In 1898, while studying at the École des Beaux-Arts in Paris, Tony Garnier (*Fig. 1*) first considered designing an imaginary industrial city. The following year Garnier won the *prix de Rome* competition for a standard Beaux-Arts project—a national bank—and was sent to the French Academy at the Villa Medici in Rome, where he began to develop his ideas on urban planning. In 1901 he sent back to the École a first study of the Cité Industrielle (*Fig. 2*). It consisted of a plan and elevation, possibly many architectural studies, and a youthful statement renouncing the traditional study of antiquity.[1] The École refused to exhibit it and ordered Garnier to produce the work on classical and Renaissance architecture which was normally required of a *pensionnaire*, or to return to Paris. But Garnier continued work on his independent project for three more years, and in 1904 he finally exhibited it in Paris at the École as supplementary work along with a more conventional study, a reconstruction of the ancient town of Tusculum.

Garnier continued work on the Cité for some time. The ultimate product of his original idea was a two-volume work (*Une Cité Industrielle*), published in 1917 in loose sheets, containing a descriptive preface (translated in our Appendix I) of great value as the main source of Garnier's thinking on the Cité (in which he mentions, among other important ideas, the utopian-socialist foundations for the city administration, and the fact that the public buildings were to be built of reinforced concrete), and 164 plates (see Appendix II for summary of contents).

To describe Garnier's Cité briefly: it was designed for an area in southeast France, situated on a plateau with high land and a lake to the north, a valley and a river to the south; and it was intended, according to Garnier, to be similar to actual towns of the area. In his presentation Garnier tried to take into account all the aspects of a real city, including governmental, cultural, residential, manufacturing, and agricultural facilities. The various functions of the city are clearly related, but separated from each other by location and circulation patterns. The city proper comprises two parts: public and residential areas. In the public area buildings are grouped into three sections: administrative services and assembly halls, museum collections, and sports and spectacle facilities. The residential area is made up of rectangular blocks running east-west, which give the city its characteristic elongated form. The city proper is connected by arterial roads to several appendages: a railroad station to the east, a large metallurgic factory to the southeast, mines east of the river that are related to the factory, an old town to the northeast, and a silk manufacturing factory to the north of the old town. Above this area is the source of the city's power, a hydroelectric station and a dam. To the southeast of the dam, above the city and sheltered by mountains, is a hospital. Between the hospital and the city is a park. To the northwest of the city is a cemetery. All these major areas are separated from each other by green belts. Areas along the riverbank and on the plateau, such as a cattle farm and a vineyard, are developed for other uses. In the plan sections of the surrounding region are rendered as regularly planted fields, indicating agricultural development. Indeed, the only elements of an actual city that are lacking are religious structures, a jail, a police station, and a law court.[2]

Little is known about the original contents of the project, or the amount of development involved in its completion.[3] The plates that were certainly added to the book after 1904 are sketches and photos of several villas constructed by Garnier near Lyons from 1909 to 1911, and six perspective views of the Cité dated 1917 (*Figs. 4, 6, 62, 67–68, 77*).[4] The drawing of the stadium (*Fig. 25*) could not have been designed before 1905, since it is based on a photograph of the Villa Borghese garden (*Fig. 27*) only published in that year.[5]

The extent of Garnier's modifications and additions to his Cité Industrielle between the first exhibition of his work in 1904 and its published version in 1917 (the form in which it is now known) remains to be considered. Although it is difficult to trace precisely the changes and influences on the work after 1904, it is possible to determine some of the alterations and additions. One method is by comparing the first plan (*Fig. 2*), exhibited at the Paris École in 1904, with the second plan (*Fig. 3*), developed between 1904 and 1917. Pawlowski has studied the differences between the two plans, especially those concerned with alterations to the center of the city (*cf. Figs. 7 and 8*) and the station quarter (*cf. Figs. 53 and 54*).[6] Chief among the changes that he notes are the removal of a covered market from the center of the city to the station quarter, where a large number of shops were added; the enlargement of the cultural facilities of the city center, including the introduction of a hall for temporary exhibitions (*Figs. 23–24*); the modification of the sports and spectacles center to accord with the Lyons stadium designed by Garnier from 1913–1918 (*Fig. 9*), and the addition of the public baths building (*Figs. 19–20*); the replacement of individual dwellings in the station quarter with four-story apartment buildings (*Figs. 47–51*), creating, apparently, a suitable high density for this area of the city (and demonstrating the already evident shift from nineteenth-century utopian ideals of individual house and garden to more economically oriented, collective twentieth-century housing); and the addition of a new primary school (*Fig. 40*) and a hotel to the station quarter. Of the two types of additional apartment buildings, one design, the group of dwellings around a central open stairway, is closely related to an interesting and still existing apartment house complex for lower-class workers built before 1906 in Paris (*Fig. 52*).

Garnier's work on projects in Lyons and the several *concours*, or competitions, to which he subsequently submitted schemes[7] must be seen as a continuation and a development of his work on the Cité Industrielle. Garnier returned to Lyons in 1905, and built there a series of civic buildings, including abattoirs (1908–1924; *Figs. 61, 63–64*), a stadium (1913–1918; *Figs. 9, 45*), and a hospital (1911–1927; *Figs. 46, 72*). He also designed several unexecuted projects for the city, including a bourse (*Fig. 12*) and a school of applied arts (*Fig. 29*), both before 1919. Revisions appear to have been made to the stadium and the abattoirs of the Cité Industrielle based on his work done at Lyons (*cf. Figs. 8 and 9, 60 and 61*). The Lyons abattoirs influenced the development of the factory area of the Cité. Work on the Lyons projects may also have influenced the Cité hospital (*Figs. 68–70*), and possibly may account for the addition of the clock tower to the Cité assembly building (*Figs. 7–8, 16*). On the other hand, work on the Cité may have been the source for several of Garnier's projected studies, namely the bourse (*cf. Figs. 10 and 12*) and the art school (*cf. Figs. 28 and 29*).

But, whatever the dates of the drawings for the Cité, the remarkable stylistic consistency of the architecture indicates that any additions after 1904 grew out of Garnier's original conceptions and do not reflect an important change in the philosophy of the work.

13

THE CONCEPT

THE LYONS BACKGROUND

Tony Garnier was born in Lyons in 1869. Pawlowski has suggested that this city and its surrounding region had a profound influence on him.[8] During Garnier's boyhood Lyons was an industrial center for textiles and metallurgy, the two industries included in the Cité. Lyons also had undergone extensive urban remodeling from the middle of the nineteenth century. Here in the 1890's projects for new public schools were begun, syndicates were formed, and a new industrial quarter was planned. Reinforced concrete was used by this time not only for industrial buildings but also for housing. Lyons' automobile industry, which was later to become so important, also was beginning to develop.[9] Although these aspects of Lyons did not appear in that city until after Garnier had left for Paris in 1889 to enter the École des Beaux-Arts, his absence from his native city, and the short visits which he probably made there during his student years, could have reinforced his impressions of the changes taking place more than constant association with the city.

Even more relevant to the Cité Industrielle was the increasing tendency then to consider Lyons as being part of a unique regional entity. In 1894 the fifteenth congress of the *Société française de géographie* met in Lyons and established a program for the region, including the construction of public utilities and dams (the latter were modeled on earlier Swiss developments in hydroelectric power). During the nineties a hydroelectric dam was being considered for the region of Lyons. Paralleling this development, Garnier stated in his preface that the siting of the Cité was determined by the location of water, the source of power. It has even been suggested that the site Garnier chose for his Cité may have been an actual, though idealized, one located on the Rhone below Lyons, and in the neighborhood of four existing cities to which Garnier related his imaginary one.[10] There may be, however, other bases for the conceptualization of his site, as will be discussed below.

URBAN REFORMS

Among the technical innovations stressed in contemporaneous thinking and reflected in Garnier's Cité Industrielle were municipal reforms of a physical and social nature. These reforms, which had been implemented by the Baron Georges Eugène Haussmann (1809–1891) in his mid-century replanning of Paris, had been developed considerably further by the end of the century. At this time in France technical and hygienic improvements, including water supply, public transportation, planting, parks, open spaces, and wide streets, were taken into consideration in city planning. In addition, the French government supported the provision of public instruction and education in technical trade schools, libraries, museums, and similar institutions.[11]

By the last quarter of the nineteenth century the study of the functional nature of city planning had shifted from France to Germany, where emphasis on sanitation and cleanliness tended to overshadow aesthetic considerations. To achieve these hygienic goals large areas were opened up to sunlight, and planting was encouraged in the interest of health. With an eye to future expansion a strict zoning of various functions of the city and stringent building laws relating to interior courts and regulating the amount of site that would be used for building, were considered to be of maximum importance.[12] In Frankfurt by 1897 considerably more than half the total area of a site for multiple dwellings had to be uncovered;[13] at Leipzig, factories, shipping yards, and railroad stations were removed from the city center and grouped together as interdependent entities.[14] In some German manufacturing cities the establishment of trade schools adapted to the industrial character of the city or vicinity aided the principal industries.[15] By the turn of the century the practical reforms popularized by Germany had spread throughout Europe. In England they were introduced by Thomas Coglan Horsfall (1841–1932).[16] In France hygienic and scientific advances were frequently discussed in current periodicals, as, for example, the orientation of rooms within dwellings for the most advantageous amount of sunlight[17]—a concern that caused Garnier to give the main section of the Cité Industrielle its characteristic elongated east-west form.

Many of these reforms were stressed by Garnier in his preface. He was emphatic about separating the functions of the city from each other in order to allow for independent expansion, functional convenience, and ease of transportation. At the same time, he excelled in organically interrelating the various components of the city; it is this characteristic more than any other which has caused come critics to consider him the first twentieth-century planner.[18] He achieved the parklike nature of his city by placing all tall buildings in one section (the railroad station quarter), by carefully zoning the area to be occupied by residences on their plots, by providing right-of-ways between houses, and by banning walls, fences, and other enclosures around these plots. Light wells were also eliminated, and the density and height of buildings were carefully regulated, not for appearance but for ideal conditions of hygiene. Garnier was concerned enough with the mechanical functioning of the city to devote three plates to outlining the drainage system for a section of the residential area (listed in our Appendix II, plates 148–150).

REGIONALISM

By the end of the nineteenth century the theory of urbanism had expanded far beyond utilitarian and geographical concerns to include the total regional context in which the city was situated. Major reports on municipal reforms in the last part of the nineteenth century were made by individuals like Albert Shaw (1857–1947) and the brothers Honoré and Elysée Reclus (1830–1905), who stressed the organic relation of the city to the country and predicted their eventual integration[19] These concepts of regionalism attained their greatest popularity in England; chief among those responsible for their development was Patrick Geddes (1854–1932). Geddes was in contact with the Reclus brothers and was possibly an influence on Garnier. Garnier's philosophy for the Cité was similar to Geddes' in the emphasis on the city's decentralization and on its being developed in relationship to the industries, occupations, and customs of the surrounding region. It is not known, however, if Garnier had firsthand knowledge of Geddes before he worked out his project. Geddes did not come to France until the Paris Exposition of 1900, two years after Garnier had conceived the Cité and more than a year after he had left for Rome. Moreover, at this time Geddes' interests were not yet focused on regionalism.

Geddes' theories are considered to be related to those expressed by Ebenezer Howard (1850–1928) with regard to his Garden City.[20] The Cité is similar in several aspects to Howard's project, which was first published in 1898. Two of Howard's basic assumptions were also stressed by Garnier: the emancipation of man from the monotony of his present labor in order to

16

take on more fruitful occupations, and the view that all men are inherently cooperative and equal. The two schemes are also related in such details as the inclusion of electric energy, the emphasis on planting within the city, and the widely accepted nineteenth-century ideal of a house and garden for each family.

However, Howard's concern with the practical economics of financing his city and his insistence on optimum density and a protective green belt were not shared by Garnier in his Cité Industrielle. And the approximation of Howard's optimum population of 32,000 to Garnier's assumption of 35,000 inhabitants, although similar, is in all probability accidental. Certainly the figures result from differing concepts of the character of a town, since Howard's has a static population and Garnier's is designed for expansion. Indeed, based on the above comparison, Garnier's project seems more technically practical, and Howard's more economically and sociologically sophisticated. Moreover, the diagrammatic character of Howard's scheme, which relates it to earlier nineteenth-century English prototypes, such as James Buckingham's Victoria, has led some critics to consider Howard's scheme less advanced than Garnier's.[21]

While it is possible that Garnier saw the first edition of Howard's book in the year that he conceived the Cité, 1898, it is more likely that his project was the result of regionalist developments in France paralleling those in England. To explore the precise connections between his Cité Industrielle and regionalist philosophy, then, it is necessary to turn to French proponents of regionalism. An important contributing factor to its development was the mid-nineteenth-century reaction in France against the dominant central role of the state and toward federalization and decentralization. Political and philosophical contributions to this movement came from Pierre-Joseph Proudhon (1809–1865), who emphasized the autonomy of industry and agriculture from one another. The cultural side of the movement was promoted at the same time by the Félibrigistes, a group concerned with the regional art and language of Provence and led by Frédéric Mistral (1830–1914).[22] Scientific contributions to the movement were made by Frédéric Le Play (1806–1882), who was responsible for the definition and scientific development of the application of geographical conditions to sociology. Le Play's study of the interrelationship of place, work, and society was influential both in France and in Britain (where Geddes was deeply indebted to Le Play for contributions to his own thought). From this background there developed in the 1880's and 1890's a complete

17

philosophy of regionalism, and by the turn of the century this thinking had become a force powerful enough to influence the political as well as the cultural sphere of French life. The regionalist movement at that time stood for preservation of provincial characteristics, for governmental decentralization, for the building of regional universities, for museums, for the conservation of historical monuments and sites, and for the encouragement of native arts and crafts and local industries.

In his preface to *Une Cité Industrielle*, Garnier specifically included most of the major elements of contemporary regionalist theory; the Cité was to represent one of a federation of cities, among which a bond would be created through emphasis on communication and the exchange of goods. Conditions of the immediate area were to be exploited. Local historical and botanical museums, exhibition buildings for regional expositions, and schools of the arts and the industries of the locality were to be included in this project. Local crafts were to be taught, and the two industries which were to be developed utilized the wealth of natural resources in the region. Nearby waterpower was to be used for transportation and for power. Finally, the deliberate proximity of the railway station to the old town, as if to make visits easier for sightseers, should be understood as an interpretation of the regionalist theory of preserving and promoting an interest in local monuments.

However, regionalism was never associated with socialism, and thus in this major philosophical tenet the Cité Industrielle does not conform to regionalist thought. Individual initiative is not stressed in the Cité; property is owned in common and public conveniences are maintained for the benefit of all. Since Lyons was strongly oriented toward socialism, it has been suggested as the source for Garnier's point of view. Garnier had lived in the workers' section of the city, and some of his later planning may reflect socialist doctrines to which he was exposed there.[23] In his Cité employment services and free hostels, as well as the many meeting rooms, were created for the workers' syndicates that a socialist government presupposes. Many public facilities were provided, equality of the sexes prevailed in education, and courts for arbitration were included as a substitution for the usual law courts. Public services, such as slaughterhouses, flour mills, a bakery, a dairy, and pharmacies, were placed under the jurisdiction of the city administration. The same administration was responsible for regulation of the dam and its electrical output, and hence heat and light for the city, as well as the more usual functions of street cleaning and other maintenance.

SOCIALIST-UTOPIAN THEORY

Modern socialist philosophy is rooted in utopian ideals of eighteenth-century thought, as, for example, expressed popularly by Jean-Jacques Rousseau (1712–1778). At the end of the nineteenth century it was believed by many social philosophers that social reforms could be achieved gradually through moral and intellectual education leading to a future ideal state. At this time there occurred a revival of the philosophy of early-nineteenth-century socialist-utopian thinkers, especially that of Charles Fourier (1772–1837); indeed, Fourierist ideals were very current by the end of the century. For instance, Émile Zola's (1840–1902) *Travail*, written contemporaneously with the planning of the Cité, was based almost solely on the earlier socialist-utopian doctrines of Fourier. Moreover, although Garnier had designed his Cité Industrielle before reading Zola's work, the two concepts were so similar (doubtless because both were infused with current Fourierist thinking) that the architect added Zola's name and the book title to a perspective rendering of the administration building (*Fig. 13*) in acknowledgment of the relationship.[24]

Garnier, like Fourier, believed in the basic goodness of man: when asked why his city contained no law court, police force, jail, or church, he is said to have replied that the new society, governed by socialist law, would have no need of churches, and that, as capitalism would be suppressed, there would be no swindlers, robbers, or murderers.[25] It can be assumed that, having omitted a church, he substituted a more "natural" form of worship, similar to the worship of nature Zola established in his *Travail*.

In utopias of this period, fundamental, natural, and primitive conditions were stressed;[26] the emphasis on exercise, health, and physical well-being was corollary to the wakening interest in natural life. Garnier's inclusion of a large public area for sports and spectacles in the Cité (*Figs. 6–8*) relates to early utopian philosophy in the late eighteenth century, which was oriented toward a more "natural" pagan antiquity, and the love of games.[27] He assumed that the ideal qualities of fraternity, goodness, and love of work were a fundamental part of man's behavior. Finally, he emphasized the industrial character of his ideal city because he felt that industry satisfied a natural or basic need to work.

New materials and technical methods played an increasingly greater role in utopian projects during the nineteenth century: for instance, André Godin (1817–1888) designed an ingenious ventilation system for his Familistère (a worker-owned factory built in Guise around 1870, and based on Fourier's concepts). Garnier also exaggerated and glorified technology for its own sake. He was extremely interested in technical details: he specified that all interior walls in the Cité were to be smooth with rounded corners,[28] and he introduced technical innovations such as straight tracks so that the trains could run faster, and a movable stage so that theatrical performances could be speeded up. Garnier's inclusion of the latest developments in electricity and reinforced concrete (see below), and the manufacture of automobiles and airplanes (both part of the metallurgic industry), must be explained partly as a utopian preoccupation with novel technical devices.

THE ARCHITECTURE

THE ÉCOLE DES BEAUX-ARTS

Tony Garnier's first architectural training was at the École Nationale des Beaux-Arts in Lyons (1885–1889); in 1889 a scholarship (the *prix Bellemain*) from the Lyons institution enabled him to study at the École Nationale Supérieure des Beaux-Arts in Paris.[29] The general academic character of both these schools influenced Garnier's development: the training at the Paris École des Beaux-Arts (1889–1899) provided the techniques which enabled Garnier to cope with the monumental and complex task of transforming his concept of an ideal city into the specific architectural rendering that we know.

The École in Paris was composed of a federation of independent smaller schools or ateliers, each presided over by an architect, or *patron*. We do not know why Garnier chose to enter the ateliers of two apparently unexceptional and traditionally oriented architects such as Paul Blondel (1847–1897) and, later, Scellier de Gisors (1844–1905) when he was admitted to the École. Possibly he was interested in the simple elevations of Scellier de Gisors' Post and Telegraph Office of 1882, in Paris, which was close to the stripped classicism that Garnier would achieve in the architecture of his Cité Industrielle. For the same reason he may also have been interested in Blondel's new Bourse of 1889, also in Paris, which replaced the simple and structurally advanced eighteenth-century Halle au Blé.[30] But neither of Garnier's *patrons* seems to have been concerned with contemporary materials, techniques, or functions, and the training they offered was probably well within the traditions of the École. On the other hand, Garnier's remarkable manifesto, submitted with the 1901 version of his Cité to the École, seems to repudiate the classical tradition of architectural education offered at the École.[31]

Garnier did, however, find a sympathetic point of view in the teaching of Julien Guadet (1834–1908), professor of architectural theory at the École. The lasting effect of Guadet's training on both Garnier and his fellow-pupil Auguste Perret (1874–1954) has been recognized.[32] Guadet's concern with rational planning, based on axiality and clear articulation of the separate parts of the building, and his interest in the relationship of architecture to contemporary functions, provided Garnier with some of the method and technical background which he would need to express his urban concepts. Indeed, the most characteristic feature of the Cité Industrielle—Garnier's clear separation of the various parts of the city based on analysis of function and circulation—must surely have been an application of Guadet's analytical method to urban planning. In its published version[33] Guadet's course at the École not only concerned itself with construction (including details of plumbing and heating, for example), but also included analyses of many civic building types that were later developed by Garnier in his Cité, such as primary schools, art and science museums, libraries, administration buildings, abattoirs, railroad stations, public baths, and theaters. These analyses were a development of the rationalistic philosophy introduced into official French architecture by Jean Louis-Nicolas Durand (1760–1834) and absorbed into French architectural thought throughout the nineteenth century. The program for the Cité hospital is close to Guadet's analysis of hospital planning, the most developed discussion of a building type in his book. Guadet favored an arrangement by separate pavilions;[34] he divided the services into facilities for patients, medicine, and surgery (including separate buildings for operations, maternity cases, baths, and hydrotherapy). He also provided consultation, or outpatient service, and a group of general facilities (kitchens, storerooms, linen, laundry, and the like), administration offices, residences, pharmacy, and a mortuary chapel—in other words, a complete program which Garnier could alter to suit the requirements of his own hospital at the Cité Industrielle (*Figs. 68–70*).

The Beaux-Arts architectural training, apart from general and practical courses,[35] consisted of a series of projects or problems (concerned with everything from the decoration of a small room to the organization of large architectural complexes) proposed by the École, to be developed by the student in his atelier as a series of examinations. There were entrance examinations; second class, first class, and diploma examinations; countless contests for medals, money, prizes; examinations every six months which eliminated many students from the École; and, above all, the annual contests for the *prix de Rome*. The manner in which the proposed problems were to be solved was set. A preliminary sketch, made without the aid of books or advice, was due within twelve hours after a project was announced for competition; a copy of this sketch, or *esquisse*, was kept by the school, and the finished design had to conform to its main ideas. In this first stage

22

of the problem reflective or original thinking was undesirable, since the emphasis was on speed; *esquisse* plans generally fell into a limited number of patterns from which further development would be facilitated.

During the ten years that Garnier spent at the École in Paris, he became expert in arriving at the essential components of any project. Garnier's six tries at the *prix de Rome* from 1894 to 1898 also further developed his ability in dealing with complex planning relationships. According to a recent critic of French academic design, Garnier's final prize-winning solution still represents a high point of the Beaux-Arts planning system.[36] His sympathy with the educational system of the École was later demonstrated in the type of art school he proposed for his industrial city. Here ateliers were placed in eleven separately housed schools, which included the various types of training offered at the Paris École: the arrangement of plaster casts in an interior hall of the École seems to have been adopted by Garnier for the hall of his projected school (*Figs. 30–31*).

Although none of the programs established by the École were urban problems—certainly none were concerned with industrial cities—the programs for several of the regular competitions, or *concours*, may have had some influence on the design of the public buildings of Garnier's Cité. Among these, the *concours Edmond Labarre* contained a wide variety of architectural programs:[37] as early as 1891 the program for a maritime railroad station was similar in its functional requirements to the one that Garnier was to develop for the station of the Cité Industrielle. In 1898 an elementary school was the problem proposed. The following year a hospital program, possibly written by Guadet, was won by Marcel Prost (b. 1874), who was to become one of France's foremost theoretical city planners; the relationship of Prost's solution (*Fig. 71*) to Garnier's later Cité Industrielle hospital design (*Fig. 68*) has been noted.[38] The details of both the *concours Labarre* and the Cité schemes are almost identical; for instance, 487 beds for Garnier's hospital and 400 for the *concours Labarre* program. Especially close is the placing of three isolated pavilions and the mortuary apart from the rest of the hospital, with the access to this special group directly from the exterior. But, unlike Prost, Garnier included additional services such as the heliotherapeutic building, the hospital for contagious diseases, and the hospital for invalids; he eliminated separate areas for men and women, and the religious appendages. Interestingly, in 1901, the year that Garnier first sent his Cité to Paris, a "People's Palace," composed of an employment center, cooperative services, theater, gymnasium, library, offices, meeting rooms, and other areas, similar in function to those of some of the public buildings which Garnier proposed for his administrative center, was proposed for the *concours Labarre*.

The *prix de reconnaissance des architectes américaines* also contained at least one program that could have been used by Garnier.[39] The 1898 program was for a central station for travelers in a capital city, and was similar to Garnier's later Cité Industrielle station (*Figs. 53–55*), especially in its requirement that the tracks be sunk or set in a viaduct. In both this 1898 program and the earlier 1891 *concours Labarre* program, a two-level station was specified: the tracks were to be on the lower level, and on the upper level in relation to the areas of arrival and departure were a waiting room, baggage rooms, offices, buffet, telegraph office, and the like. All were areas similar to those proposed in Garnier's program in developing his own station.

Garnier's special interest in nature was expressed in his prize-winning solution of 1896 for a zoological garden for the *concours Labarre* and his botanical garden for the *concours Chenavard* of 1895 (*Fig. 43*). This interest persisted, for instance, in Garnier's design for an enclosed patio in a residence of the Cité (*Fig. 42*), as well as in his constant enthusiasm for the elements of a park-like setting in his city.

But the educational program of the École may have exerted less influence on the student Garnier than did the composition of the student body. The policy of admission to the École ensured a diverse character to this group, since instruction was offered without charge, and the school was open to any candidate who could pass the examinations. During the 1890's a group of radical students, including Garnier, who were concerned with new social values and were interested in problems of planning as related to these values, began to contribute to the atmosphere of the École. We have seen that by 1901 the École's official position, as exemplified in the *concours Labarre*, reflected this interest. Prior to Garnier's Cité the outstanding expression of this trend was the project for "A People's Center in the Metropolis of a Great Democratic State" submitted in 1900 to the *concours Chenavard* by Léon Jaussely (b. 1875).[40]

Although Jaussely's project was executed in the typical Beaux-Arts style, the program he attached to it reads like

Garnier's own socialist-utopian preface to his *Une Cité Indus-trielle:*

> The progress and application of science and modern tech-nology will modify the present composition of society (allow-ing man more independence and leisure)—advancing human-ity toward the realization of spiritual liberation through social education.
>
> In each city some large place should be created where citizens will be able not only to expand their education, but also to discuss the organization and conditions of their work, and to hold demonstrations freely.
>
> In the metropolis of a great democratic state that is truly worthy of this title, these new functions require durable, utilitarian, and humanitarian structures expressing the pro-gress of mankind.

Jaussely's choice of public buildings (a "people's palace," a popular university, a library, an industrial arts school, a popular theater, museums for permanent and temporary exhibitions, pub-lic baths and swimming pools, a gymnasium, and the like) is also similar to that of Garnier's city center which consists of adminis-tration and sports and spectacles facilities. Indeed, Garnier, pos-sibly inspired by the earlier project, included in his center for a medium-sized city enough building types to have supported the civic needs of a large metropolis like the one for which Jaussely designed his center.

The People's Center was not the only program of this nature. In the same year, 1900, just before Garnier submitted his Cité Industrielle to the École for the first time, Joseph Duquesne (b. 1868) sent to the École a project for a Maison du Peuple as part of his second-year work in Rome.[41] Moreover, Marcel Prost (b. 1874) and Eugène Hébrard (b. 1875), both progressive ur-banists, also attended the École at this time, and Jaussely's well-known project for Barcelona was schematically very close to Garnier's Cité (*cf. Figs. 80 and 81*): both contain cities on a plain between a body of water and mountains, industry next to the water, housing above, separated from industry by a railroad and surrounding an adminstration center, and a hospital at the highest point, with cemeteries to the side. Jaussely's project was designed in 1903 at the French Academy in the Villa Medici during Garnier's residence there.

THE VILLA MEDICI

During the period that Garnier was at the Villa Medici (1900–1904), a rash of reconstructions of ancient cities was in preparation to be sent back to Paris from the French Academy at Rome; the most important were Jean Hulot's work on Selinus (begun in 1903), Marcel Prost's on Constantinople (envoi of 1905), and Eugène Bigot's study of ancient Rome (begun in 1902).[42] Garnier, too, worked on an ancient city project for official credit when he was sent to Rome, the reconstruction of the ancient Roman city of Tusculum.[43] Although it has been suggested that the work of Hulot, Prost, and Bigot was inspired by the example of Garnier's earlier Tusculum project,[44] it is more likely that all of these projects may be related to the other work on ancient sancturaries previously begun at the Villa Medici and later published from 1889 on: Victor Laloux' *Olympia*, Alphonse Defrasse's *Epidaurus*, and Emmanuel Pontremoli's *Pergamum*.[45]

In spite of official disapproval (discussed in our Introduction above), Garnier spent most of his four years as a *prix de Rome* scholar working on his project for a modern city. Yet, not surprisingly, some of the architecture of the Cité Industrielle is related to the architectural remains of antiquity and to reconstructions by the *anciens pensionnaires*. Even the general site of the Cité is reminiscent of the acropolis of a Hellenistic city such as Pergamum, which also rises above a plain (*cf. Figs. 4 and 5*). The roadway that spans the declivities of the plain is similar in form to Roman aqueducts. And Garnier's dam can be compared in its scalloped form and the function of its retaining wall to the type of concrete design to be found in Roman cisterns and the ruined niched walls which Garnier could have seen while at the Villa Medici (*cf. Figs. 76 and 77*).[46]

The most specific reference in the Cité to antique forms, and the only one which Garnier himself stated that he had derived from antiquity (our Appendix I), was the outdoor theater, which, although not illustrated by Garnier but included by him in his general city plan (*Figs. 2–3*), was modeled on the Greek theater; a similar theater was preserved in Tusculum. Several of his other designs also appear to have been derived from ancient architecture. The temporary exhibition hall of the Cité is similar to the Altar of Zeus at Pergamum, based on a reconstruction of the Altar made by Pontremoli in his study of Pergamum already mentioned (*cf. Figs. 22 and 23*): both are rectangular structures with stairways at their four corners running along the long sides. And one

26

of the houses of the Cité Industrielle has a Roman atrium complete with impluvium that could have been taken directly from a Roman house of Herculaneum or Pompeii (*Fig. 44*). The relation of his public baths building to thermae of Imperial Rome can, however, be considered to be more a part of prevailing architectural tradition in Europe than of deliberate borrowing by Garnier.

STRUCTURE

Beyond the brief comments in periodicals about his schoolwork that are cited in our Bibliography, nothing is known to date of Garnier's years at the École. We do know that he was poor, and it is possible that in order to support himself he worked for a firm where he would have been exposed to the most recent developments in structural techniques and new materials. There is no doubt that while at the École Garnier was aware of contemporary building developments. Chief among these developments was the growing use of reinforced concrete which was beginning to compete with metal during the last years of the nineteenth century and which became the major structural material of the 1900 Paris Exposition. It began to be used more widely after construction was begun in 1894 on Anatole de Baudot's church of Saint-Jean de Montmartre in Paris (*Fig. 11*). This was the first monumental building in which reinforced concrete was used as a light, visible skeleton, although the system was not fully developed, and was in part dependent on brick masonry.[47]

This material must have been attractive to Garnier because of its association with utopian thought of the late nineteenth century. Contemporary architectural publications heralded it as the material of the future.[48] As soon as new systems of its use appeared they were published by the press, which assumed this complex material to be the answer to many previously unsolved building problems. Baudot claimed that reinforced concrete would completely alter the function and purpose of architecture[49] Conversely, the conception of a return to a previous simpler and more natural type of construction may be related to the idea of the material as being associated with more traditional masonry construction.[50]

Much of Garnier's information about reinforced concrete may have come from reading about the material in contemporary periodicals; for instance, the idea of rounding corners of interior spaces to eliminate dust and to make cleaning easier was first mentioned in a periodical and then included by Garnier in his preface, as we have seen.[51] Both the idealization of the potentialities of this material, and the association of it with older, more fundamental structural traditions by the periodicals and other contemporaneous publications reflecting current architectural theory, would make it a logical choice for Garnier to use in his Cité Industrielle. That he was interested in the utopian rather than the practical aspects of concrete seems evident since in spite of the fact that his entire project was constructed of this material, his publication of the Cité contains no technical data on concrete, except for several plates of photographs showing concrete construction with no explanatory titles. Indeed, in his preface, except for brief mention of economy, Garnier was concerned only with aesthetic uses of reinforced concrete. These were that the simplicity of its construction allows for the arrangement of decorative ornaments to their best advantage, an outstanding example being the oversized Nike statue placed before several simple, small houses (*Fig. 39*), and that an architectural style of long horizontals and verticals (based on Garnier's favored forms in reinforced concrete) is in conformity with the simplicity of "natural" forms (*Figs. 24, 73*).[52]

The reinforced concrete system could be developed both as a continuation of the traditional post and lintel method employed in stone and wood construction, or as a monolithic unit of forms flowing together with no clear separation of parts.[53] Both manners were employed by Garnier (*Figs. 18, 24*). Indeed, in his use of concrete Garnier imitated many current structural developments. The simplified and abstracted classicizing ornament of his assembly building (*Fig. 10*), for instance, paralleled Baudot's use of simplified and abstracted medievalizing ornament in Saint-Jean de Montmartre (*Fig. 11*). The idea of elevating the building on piers (*Fig. 13*) may be derived from other early work in reinforced concrete (*Fig. 15*). Even the Eiffel Tower is similar to the station tower (*cf. Figs. 55 and 56*). Parenthetically, the metal construction of the Galerie des Machines at the 1889 Paris International Exposition seems to be reflected in the metal truss design for the factory building of the Cité (*Figs. 65, 66*).

Responsibility for the popularization of reinforced concrete may be due in large part to the work of the builder François Hennebique (1843–1921).[54] His post and beam system (*Fig. 14*), which combined many of the previous pioneer contributions and emphasized the use of stirrups and continuous reinforcing, was widely known due to his extensive promotion of his work in his periodical *Le Béton armé* and his designs for the buildings at the Paris Exposition in 1900. Modified versions of the Hennebique system were widely used throughout Europe. Hennebique claimed two main advantages to reinforced concrete: economy of construction and simplicity of design. Both were to be achieved by the exclusive use of reinforced concrete and reinforced glass. There can be no doubt that the inclusion of reinforced glass with reinforced concrete in Garnier's section on construction in his preface was strongly influenced by Hennebique's work. For instance, both concrete and glass were used in the Cité railroad station (*Fig. 55*). The flared junction of the columns with the beams in Garnier's projects for the public baths (*Fig. 21*) and the assembly building (*Fig. 10*) resemble the Hennebique system (*Fig. 14*). The unusual dome of Garnier's theater appears to have been the further development of a type of dome designed for the Brunner Bank in Brussels and published in *Le Béton armé* in 1903 (*cf. Figs. 17 and 18*); it is also similar to a dome designed by Hennebique for the Museum of Egyptian Antiquities in Cairo.[55] Although Hennebique designed roof terraces for his much-publicized house at Bourg-la-Reine, built in 1904 (*Fig. 75*), roof terraces seem to have been popular in other architectural designs such as the Paris Automobile Club (*Fig. 41*),[56] and it has been pointed out that they were used in low-income housing in Lyons at this time.[57] All of these sources, as well as indigenous Mediterranean architecture, may have influenced Garnier in his choice of roof terraces for buildings of the Cité Industrielle (e.g. in *Fig. 40*).

Sources also seem to have been available for four buildings from the Cité Industrielle which previously have been considered, generally on the assumption that they were designed in 1904, to be examples of Garnier's prophetic structural vision.[58] Of these designs, that of the railroad station (*Fig. 55*) is best known; the unrealistic thinness of the light cantilevers and their supports is unique among Cité Industrielle buildings, and, indeed, even among the bulk of reinforced concrete structures built by 1917, the outside date at which designs could have been included in the published version of the Cité Industrielle. However, its work is similar to that of a structure by Hennebique for the 1900 Paris International Exposition (*Fig. 57*), which Garnier could have seen before it was covered with finishing materials, and to such experiments in reinforced concrete design as the cantilevered balcony exhibited at an exhibition in Lille, published in 1902 in *Le Béton armé* (*Fig. 58*).[59]

The heliotherapeutic building (*Figs. 73–74*) has been considered advanced because of its simple, repetitive module, its large expanse of window area, *brise-soleils*, and set-backs. Its modular design, however, may be an application of Gaudet's system of rational planning to a building composed of similar units; its set-backs may derive from the terraced set-backs of Hennebique's house (*Fig. 75*); and the large expanse of glass is surely related to Hennebique's promotion of the use of reinforced glass as a curtain wall.

The stadium (*Fig. 25*) occasionally has been included in this group because of its extensive roof cantilever. But the cantilever is similar to that of an 1898 project by M. Dontant for a hippodrome constructed of more traditional building materials (*Fig. 26*).[60] Garnier may have been inspired directly by its publication in 1898, or by similar projects.

The last of these "progressive" designs is that of the factory furnaces (*Fig. 67*). Here our interest is centered not on novel structural solutions, but on the seemingly futurist patterns produced by multilevel circulation levels, towering terracotta furnace flues, and high metal catwalks, all set against the mountainous natural background and the dam. However, it is probable that this rendering is simply an idealized version by Garnier of contemporary factories which he had seen.

POWER

The use of electricity, like reinforced concrete, figured largely in utopias during the early years of its development. By the end of the nineteenth century this form of power was associated with the future mastery of the machine and with the emancipation of man from mechanical labor; a revulsion against the dirt and waste of early manufacturing towns placed this "clean" source of power high on the list of essential innovations for the nineteenth-century reformer. The development of interest in electricity is recorded in the great exhibitions late in the century. The first international exhibition of electricity was held in Paris in 1881.[61] In the 1900 Paris Exposition electricity assumed an important role; there was an Electrical Building, and a "Château d'Eau," composed of colored lights playing on a wall of water at night, was the center of attention. The practical application of this power was highlighted by the first satisfactory installation of a hydroelectric plant at Geneva in 1895. This was hailed by architectural periodicals as the solution to problems related to the manufacture and use of electricity,[62] and many future installations were predicted. A similar hydroelectric plant was included in the Cité Industrielle.

30

THE PLAN

THE PLANNING TRADITION AT THE
TURN OF THE CENTURY

At the beginning of the twentieth century two major European planning styles prevailed: one continued the traditional formal planning exemplified by Haussmann's design for Paris, and the other carried out newer, informal planning as suggested by Camillo Sitte (1843–1903) in his *City Building According to Artistic Principles*.[63] Garnier adopted the first of these styles for the general layout of his Cité, as would be expected of an École student as well as of a Frenchman who grew up in this formal planning tradition. The major remodeling of Lyons, accomplished by Vaïse, prefect of the Rhone between 1853 and 1864, was based on the replanning of Paris.[64] This planning consisted of a rigorous application of geometric shapes, symmetry, and long, straight avenues terminating in vistas. Although compared with the complex network planning of Paris, the road system of the Cité is simple, it maintains the French tradition of long, straight streets, points, axes, and bilateral symmetry. The Cité's clock tower (*Fig. 16*) projects into the center of the major street to form a focus and terminating point for an axial vista, and public buildings are given symmetrical plans. The nonfunctional placement of the diagonal streets is also part of the Haussmann tradition. Furthermore, Garnier may have conceived the unprecedented plan of the assembly hall (*Figs. 7–8*) for axial emphasis. Finally, a parklike setting for the city is produced by the planting of trees along important streets in a manner similar to the Haussmann method of the mid-century.

Because Sitte's work was not translated into French until 1902, it is doubtful that Garnier was influenced directly by the book in the planning of the Cité Industrielle. But Sitte's book represents a general tendency in planning that can also be assumed for Garnier. A more picturesque treatment in reaction to the previous grid pattern was introduced in the planning style connected with the work of Sitte. Dramatic, unexpected aspects in planning design were stressed, which were meant to be achieved by means of short or broken streets and less isolated and symmetrical arrangement of buildings. Although for the vehicular routes of the Cité Garnier adopted the academic system to which Sitte was opposed, like Sitte he was concerned with making the city more natural by means of the beautiful setting in which it was to be placed. And in his layout of the informal pedestrian routes of the Cité (*Figs. 32–39*) Garnier achieved an effect similar to that of Sitte's irregular street patterns. Moreover, even the axial vistas and other hallmarks of the academic system were used by Garnier to break the monotony of the grid system. And, finally, characteristic of both men was the re-creation of a classical spirit that could be related to contemporary life. Garnier used a classicizing architectural vocabulary and antique building types; Sitte recommended a walk through the ruins of Pompeii as convincing proof of his thesis.

PLANNING RELATED TO THE CITÉ

If the formal characteristics of Garnier's planning seem to be a synthesis of these two opposing traditions, his Cité Industrielle is also a part of its immediate environment, and a discussion of two fairly contemporaneous plans, one in Germany, one in America, will demonstrate that the aesthetic position of the Cité Industrielle's plan was not unique. Publication of Sitte's book in 1889 caused a split in German planning: one group of planners continued to enlarge and even exaggerate the informal planning advocated by Sitte, the other reevaluated the classical and academic tradition. Otto Wagner (1841–1918), whose classicizing theories soon competed with the picturesque ideals of Sitte, belonged to the latter group. Close parallels to Garnier's Cité Industrielle can be found in Wagner's and related academic schemes.

Wagner's first studies for the replanning of Vienna date from the 1890's, though the major portion of his scheme (*Fig. 78*) was designed in the first decade of the twentieth century.[65] His conception of the city contained a series of rectangular blocks of apartments, broken at regular intervals by small parks and related to a central municipal area that is set in a large rectangular park. There could be no stronger reaction to the informality and freedom of Sitte's planning than this classicism with its emphasis on axes, long streets, and formal planting. Wagner continued Sitte's interest in the aesthetic disposition of architectural monuments within the city, but to Wagner only the practical could be beautiful, and never what was picturesque for its own sake.[66] It is to be regretted that Garnier did not share Wagner's desire to communicate his theories, for we have little written evidence by which to compare the two men. However, in Garnier's completed work the functional aspects, which are of prime importance, are nevertheless considered in terms of aesthetic expression: his relation of the architectural forms, through their simplicity, to

32

1. Commemorative medal for Tony Garnier.

2. Cité Industrielle, plan, 1901–1904.

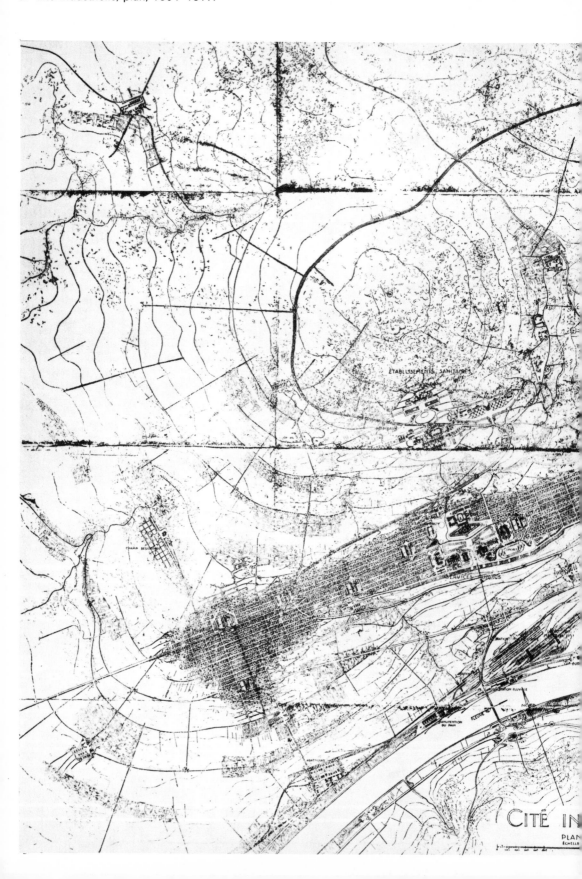

4. Cité Industrielle, view, dated 1917.

5. Pergamum, view, reconstructed by Pontremoli, 1900.

6. Cité Industrielle, city center, view, dated 1917.

7. City center, detail from plan of 1901–1904.

8. City center, detail from plan of 1904–1917.

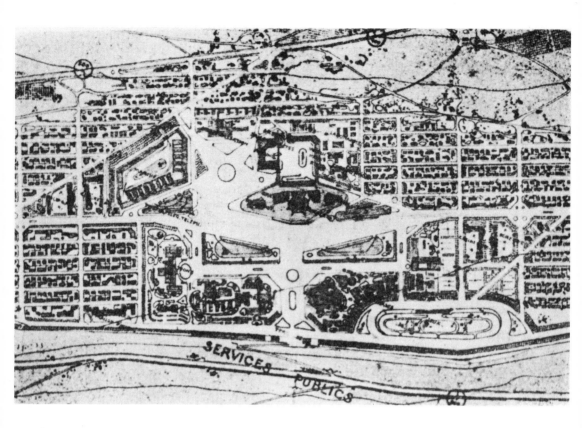

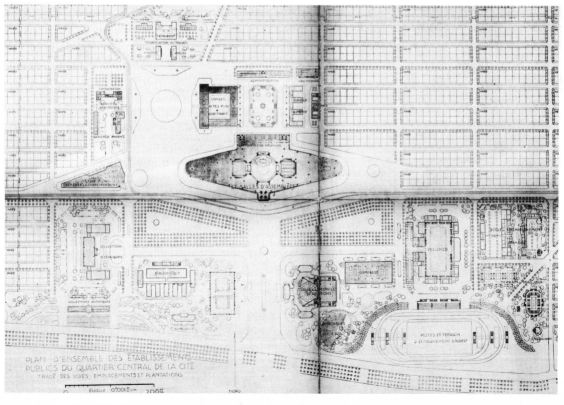

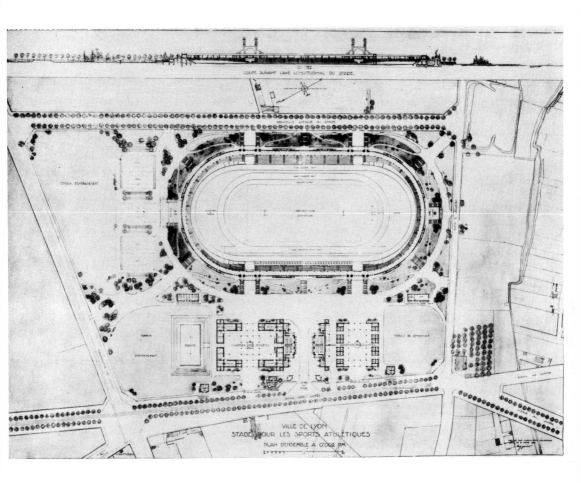

10. Cité Industrielle, assembly rooms, view.

11. Anatole de Baudot: Saint-Jean de Montmartre, interior, Paris, 1894.

12. Project for a bourse, Lyons, 1919.

13. Cité Industrielle, assembly rooms, portico.

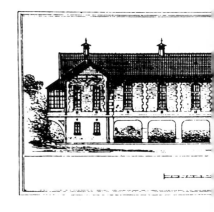

14. François Hennebique: structural system in reinforced concrete.

15. M. L. Muller: project for a hospital, Aix, 1899.

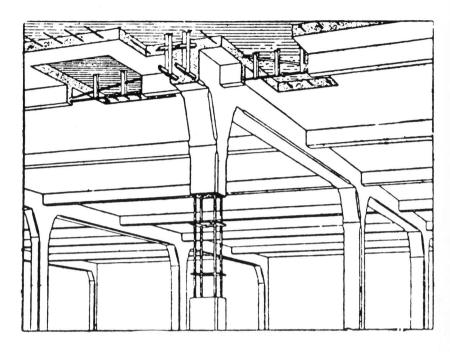

PAVILLONS DE CHIRVRGIE   COUPE

20   30   40   50   60 m

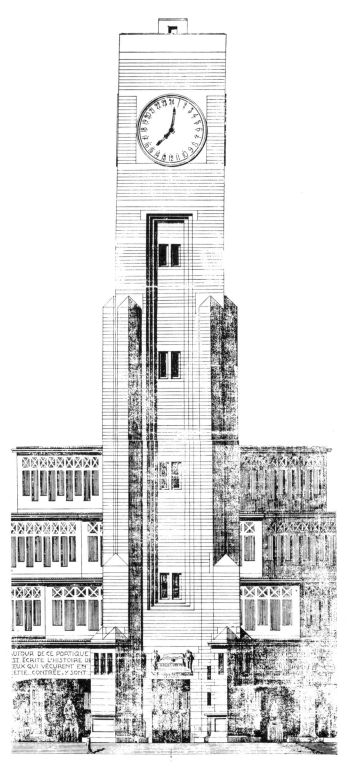

AUTOUR DE CE PORTIQUE
ST ÉCRITE L'HISTOIRE DE
EUX QUI VÉCURENT EN
ETTE CONTRÉE, Y SONT

SALLES D'ASSEMBLÉES
DÉTAIL · ÉLÉVATION
ÉCHELLE 0.m02 CPM

0   5   10 M

17. M. Geraerts: bank for Brunner and Company, dome, Brussels, c. 1900.

18. Cité Industrielle, theater, view.

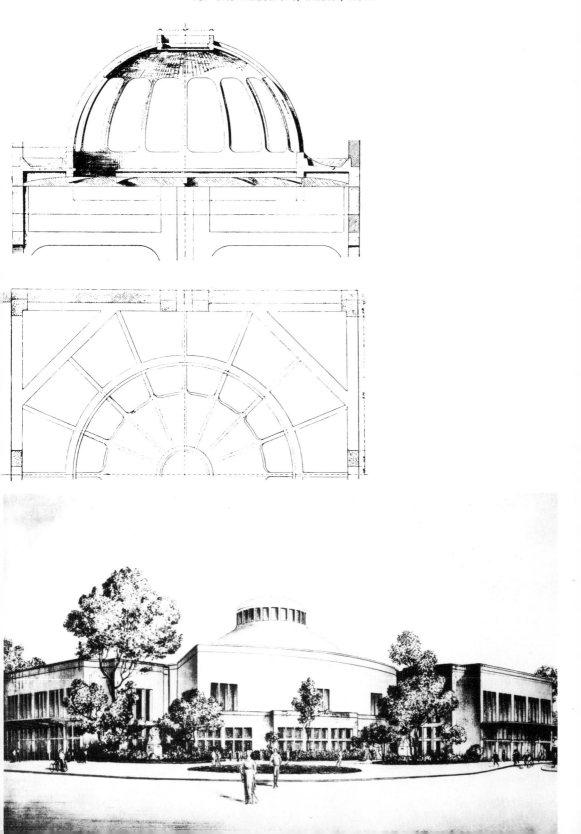

19. Cité Industrielle, public baths, elevation.

20. Public baths, plan.

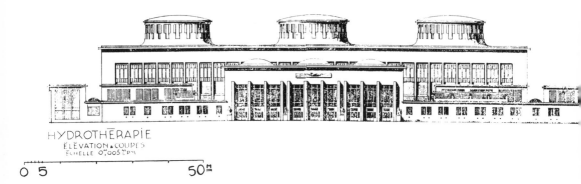

HYDROTHÉRAPIE
ÉLÉVATION & COUPES
ÉCHELLE 0ᵐ005 P M
0 5   50ᵐ

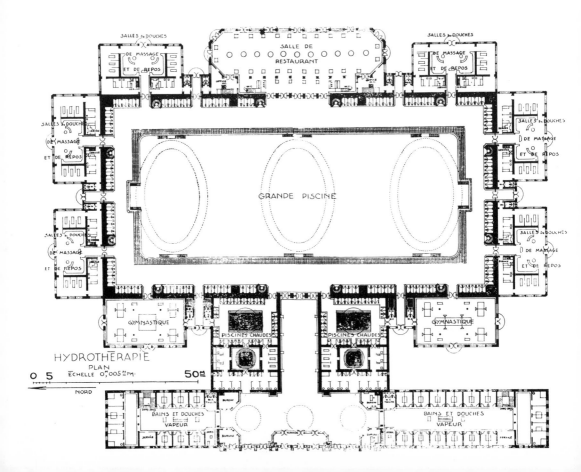

HYDROTHÉRAPIE
PLAN
ÉCHELLE 0ᵐ005 P M.
0 5   50ᵐ
NORD

22. Pergamum, Altar of Zeus, reconstructed by Pontremoli, 1900.

23. Cité Industrielle, temporary exhibition hall, plan.

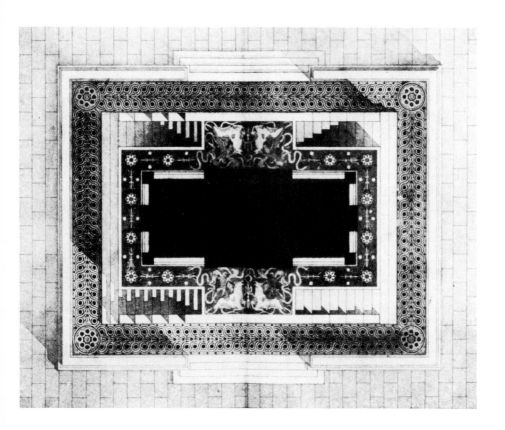

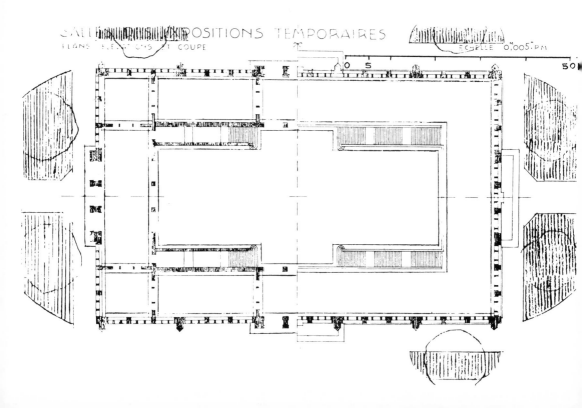

25. Cité Industrielle, stadium and training track, view.

26. M. Dontant: section of tribune, Champ de Dieppe, c. 1898.

27. Villa Borghese, amphitheater, Rome. Date of publication of photograph, 1905.

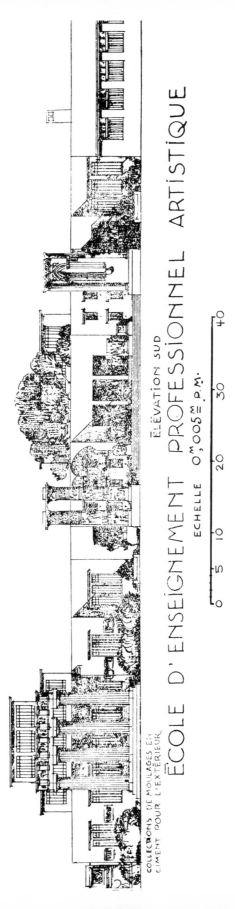

COLLECTIONS DE MOULAGES EN
CIMENT POUR L'EXTÉRIEUR

ÉLÉVATION SUD

ÉCOLE D'ENSEIGNEMENT PROFESSIONNEL ARTISTIQUE

ECHELLE O^m,OO5^m = P.M.

0   5   10   20   30   40

28. Cité Industrielle, art school, elevation.

29. Project for school of applied arts, view, Lyons, c. 1919.

30. Cité Industrielle, art school, main hall.

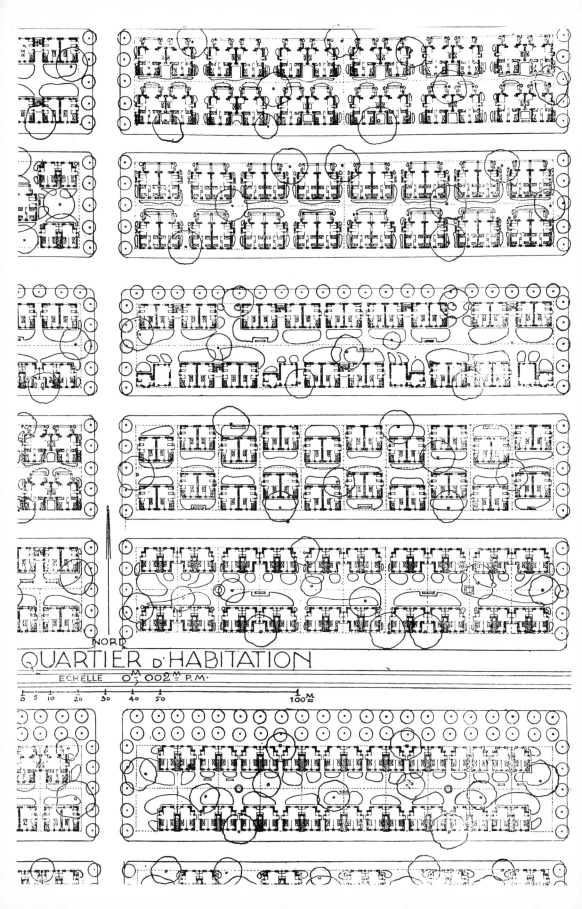

QUARTIER D'HABITATION

ECHELLE   0,002 P.M.

NORD

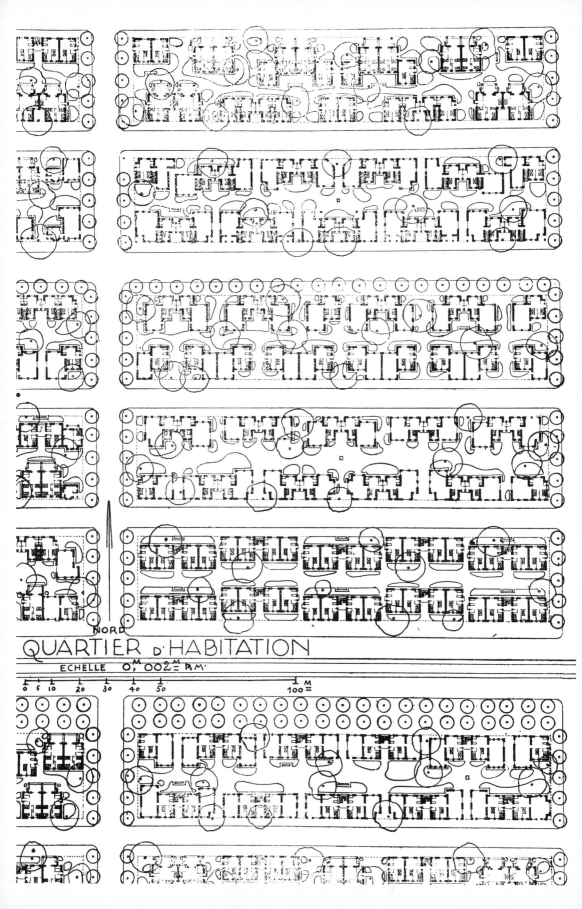

QUARTIER D'HABITATION

NORD

ECHELLE 0,M 002 = P.M.

0 5 10   20   30   40   50   100 M

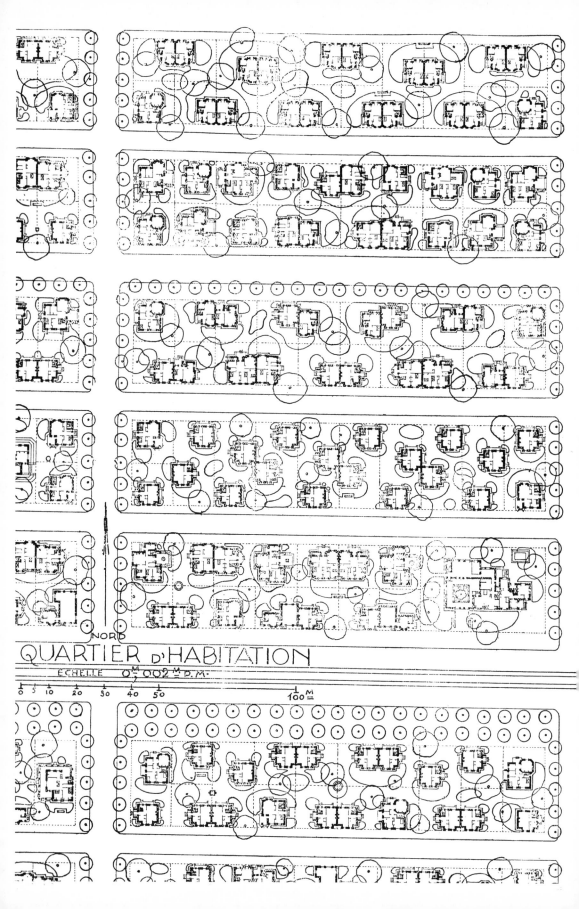

QUARTIER D'HABITATION

ECHELLE 0ᴹ002ᴹ ᴰ·ᴹ·

0 5 10   20   30   40   50   100ᴹ

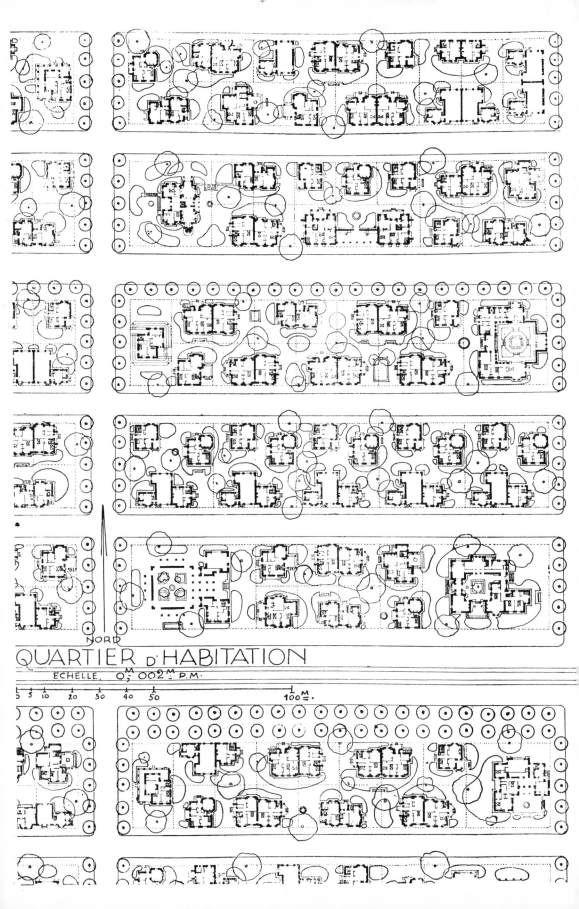

QUARTIER D'HABITATION

ECHELLE. 0,002 P.M.

NORD

40 Cité Industrielle: primary school view

41. Automobile Club, roof terrace, Paris, c. 1899.

42. Cité Industrielle house, enclosed patio.

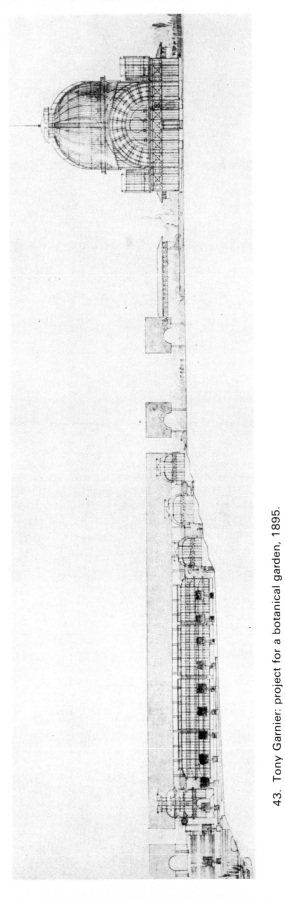

43. Tony Garnier: project for a botanical garden, 1895.

45. Municipal stadium, athletes' section, Lyons, 1913–1918.

46. Hospital of the Grange-Blanche, Lyons, 1911–1927.

47. Cité Industrielle, residential quarters, plan.

48. Cité Industrielle, apartment houses, view.

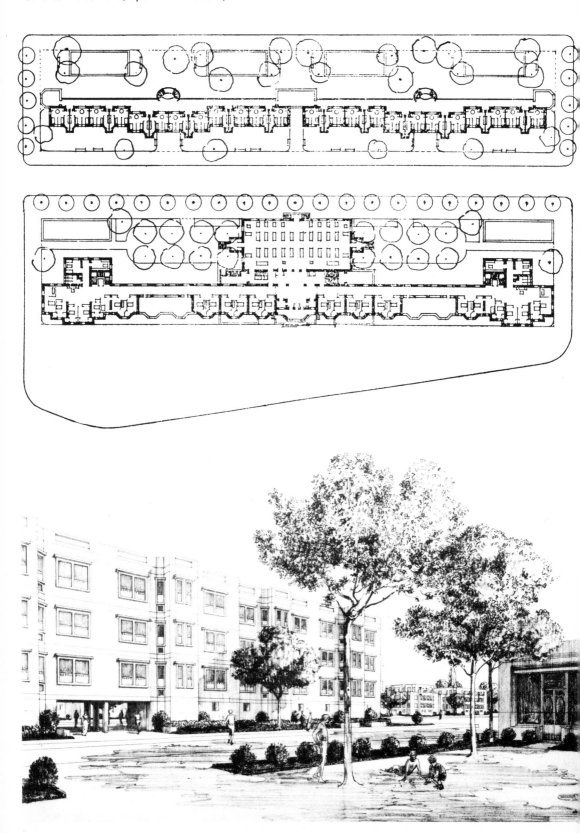

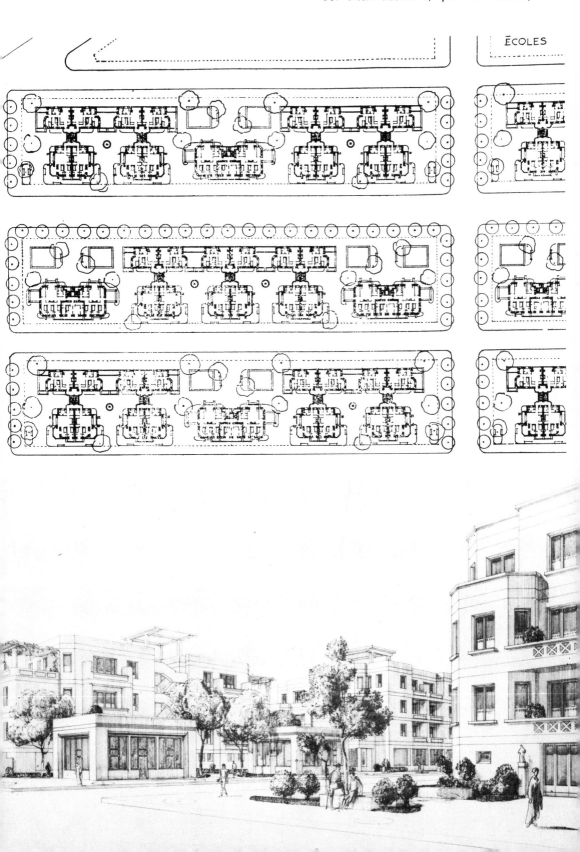

ÉCOLES

51. Apartment houses, perspective.

52. Laboussiere: apartment houses, Paris, c. 1905–1906. View showing exterior stairway.

53. Cité Industrielle, station quarter, detail from plan of 1901–1904.

54. Station quarter, detail from plan of 1904–1917.

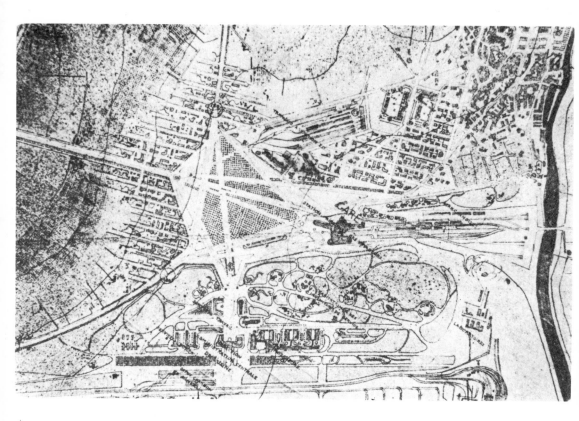

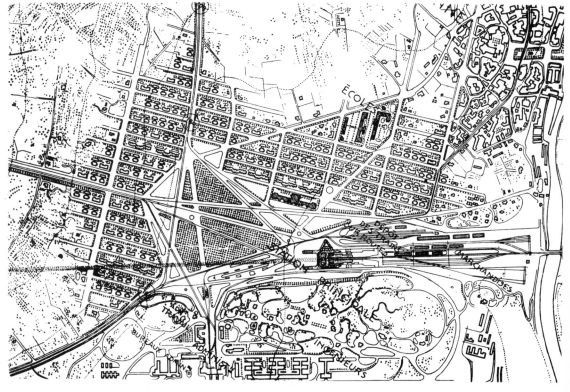

56. Gustave Eiffel: Eiffel Tower, Paris, 1889.

57. Palais des lettres, sciences et arts, Paris International Exposition, 1900. View of construction.

58. Platform, Lille, Exposition, c. 1902.

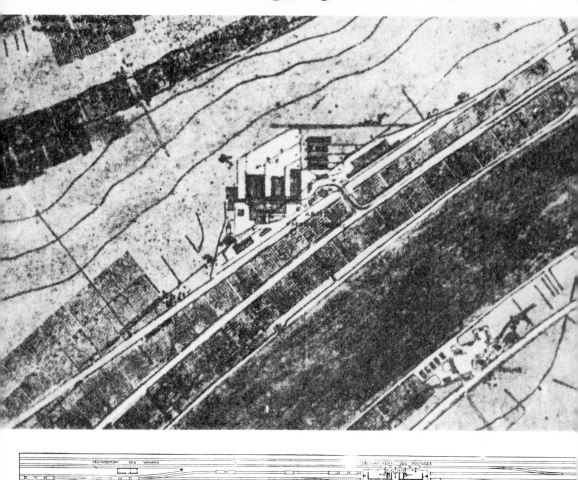

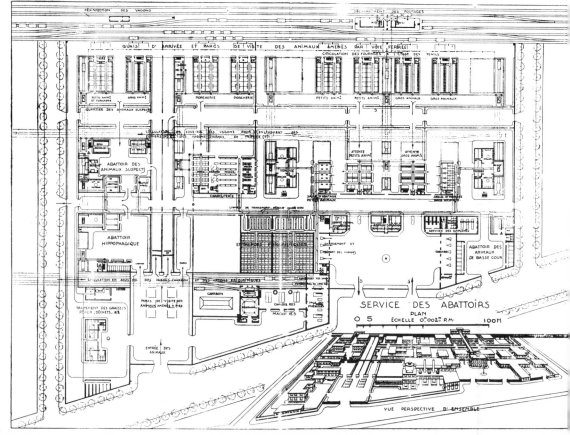

DÉSINFECTION DES VAGONS

DÉCHARGEMENT DES FOURRAGES

QUAIS D'ARRIVÉE ET PARCS DE VISITE DES ANIMAUX AMENÉS PAR VOIE FERRÉE

CIRCULATION DES FOURRAGES   ÉTAGE DES FENILS

PETITS ANIM.
ET FOURAGES   GROS ANIM.   PORCHERIE   PORCHERIE   PETITS ANIM.   PETITS ANIM.   GROS ANIMAUX   GROS ANIMAUX

QUARTIER DES ANIMAUX SUSPECTS

CIRCULATION EN SOUS-SOL DES VAGONS POUR L'ENLÈVEMENT DES
PETITS ET GROS VAGONS CITERNES ET VOITURE CRD

ATTENTE
PETITS ANIM.   ATTENTE
GROS ANIM.

ABATTOIR DES
ANIMAUX SUSPECTS

CHARCUTERIE

SALLE D'ABATAGE
DES PETITS ANIMAUX   SALLE D'ABATAGE
GROS ANIMAUX

LIGNE DE TRANSPORT AÉRIEN

ABATTOIR
HIPPOPHAGIQUE

ENTREPOTS FRIGORIFIQUES

ADMINISTRATION   SERVICES DES EMPLOYÉS

ABATTOIR DES
ANIMAUX
DE BASSE COUR

CIRCULATION EN SOUS-SOL DES VAGONS-CHARBON ET DES VAGONS FRIGORIFIQUES

PARCS DE VISITE DES
ANIMAUX AMENÉS À PIED

CHARBON

CHAUDIÈRES
MACHINES

SERVICE DES ABATTOIRS
PLAN
0 5   ÉCHELLE 0,0027 P.M.   100M

TRAITEMENT DES GRAISSES
PEAUX DÉCHETS &c

ENTRÉE DES
ANIMAUX

VUE PERSPECTIVE D'ENSEMBLE

59. Cité Industrielle, abattoirs, detail from plan of 1901–1904.

60. Abattoirs.

61. Abattoirs de la Mouche, interior, Lyons, 1908–1924.

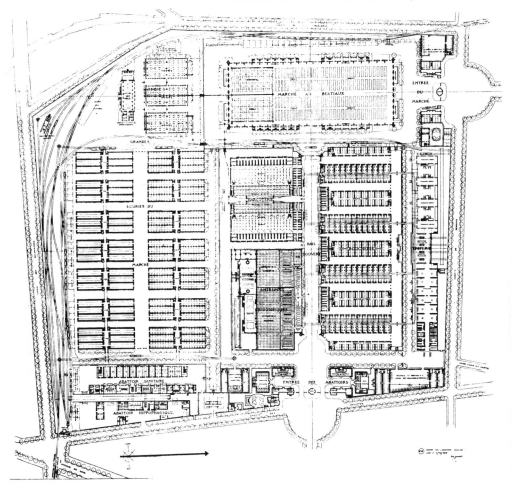

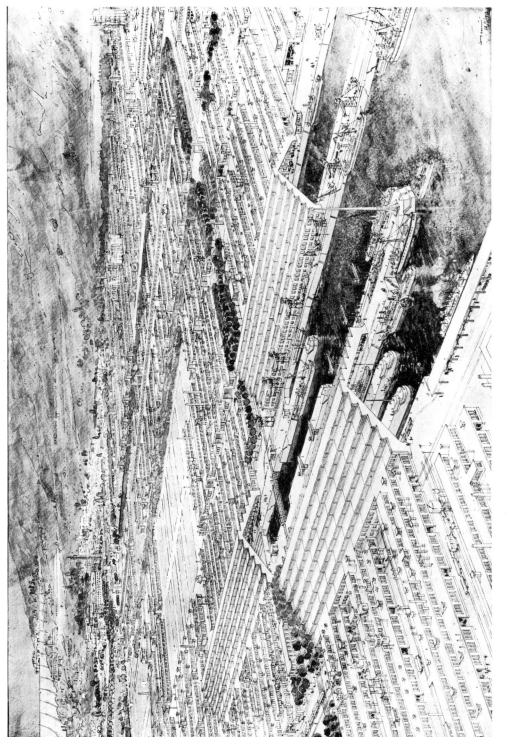

62. Cité Industrielle, factory, view, dated 1917.

63. Abattoirs de la Mouche, view, Lyons, 1908—1924.

64. Abattoirs de la Mouche, Lyons, 1908–1924. Exterior (above) and
   interior (below).

65. Cité Industrielle, factory, detail of construction.

66. Dutert and Contamin: Galerie des Machines, Paris International
   Exposition, 1889.

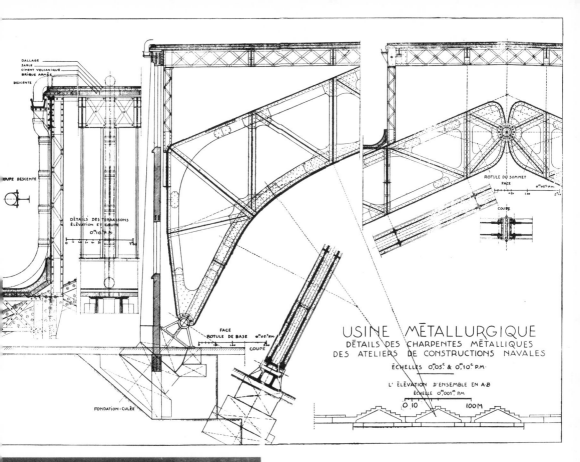

DALLAGE
SABLE
CIMENT VOLCANIQUE
BRIQUE ARMÉE

DESCENTE

COUPE DESCENTE

DÉTAILS DES TERRASSONS
ÉLÉVATION ET COUPE
0",10 P.M.

FACE
ROTULE DE BASE   0",05 P.M.

COUPE

FONDATION-CULÉE

ROTULE DU SOMMET
FACE   0",05 P.M.

COUPE

USINE MÉTALLURGIQUE
DÉTAILS DES CHARPENTES MÉTALLIQUES
DES ATELIERS DE CONSTRUCTIONS NAVALES
ÉCHELLES 0",05 & 0",10 P.M.

L' ÉLÉVATION D'ENSEMBLE EN A·B
ÉCHELLE 0",001 P.M.

0 10   100M

67. Cité Industrielle, furnaces, view, dated 1917.

68. Cité Industrielle, hospital, view, dated 1917.

70. Hospital, detail from plan of 1904–1917.

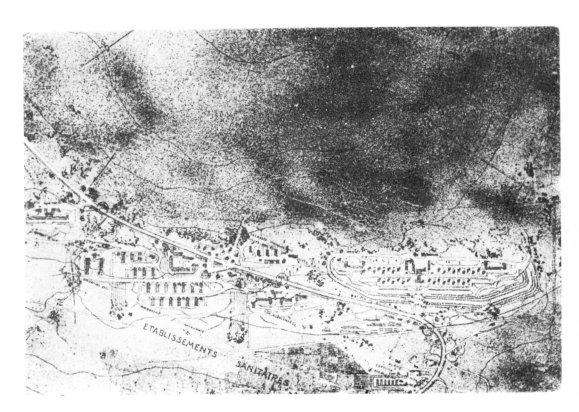

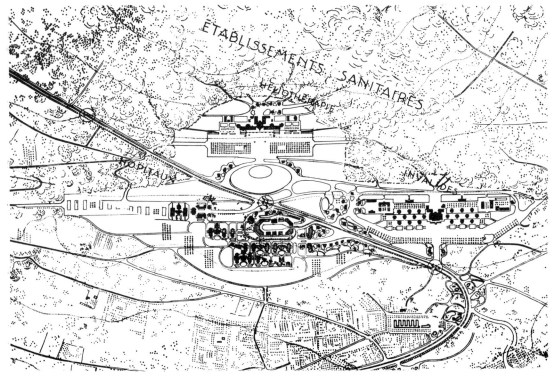

71. Marcel Prost: project for a hospital, 1899.

72. Hospital of the Grange-Blanche, plan, ground floor, Lyons, 1911-1927.

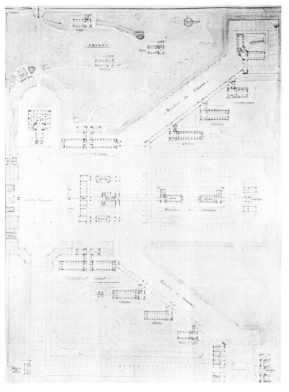

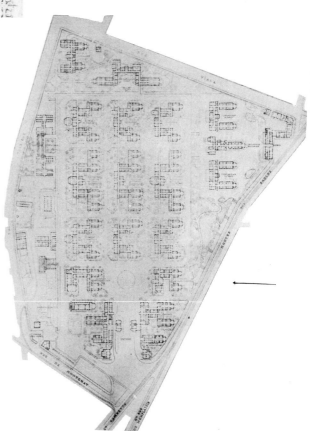

. Cité Industrielle, heliotherapeutic building, view.

74. Heliotherapeutic building, section.

75. François Hennebique: house, section, Bourg-la-Reine, 1904.

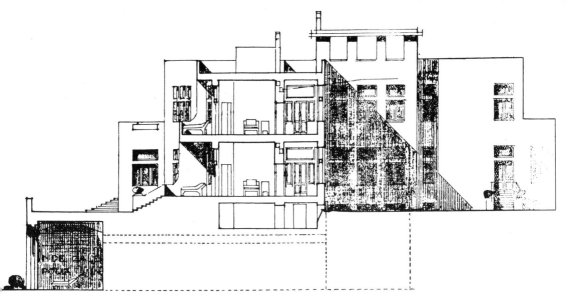

COUPE SUD-NORD SUR LES CHAMBRES

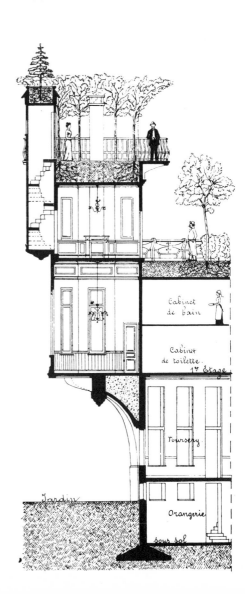

76. Villa le Vignacce, cistern, plan, Rome.

77. Cité Industrielle, dam, view.

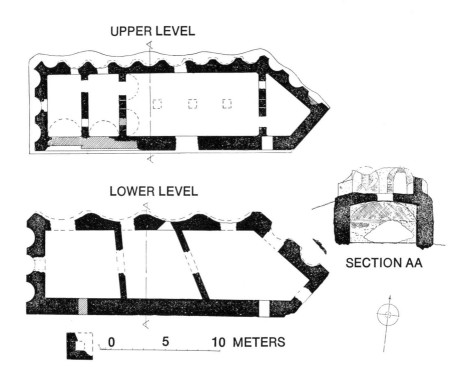

UPPER LEVEL

LOWER LEVEL

SECTION AA

0   5   10 METERS

78. Otto Wagner: project for an urban center, Vienna, 1911.

79. World's Columbian Exposition, Chicago, 1893.

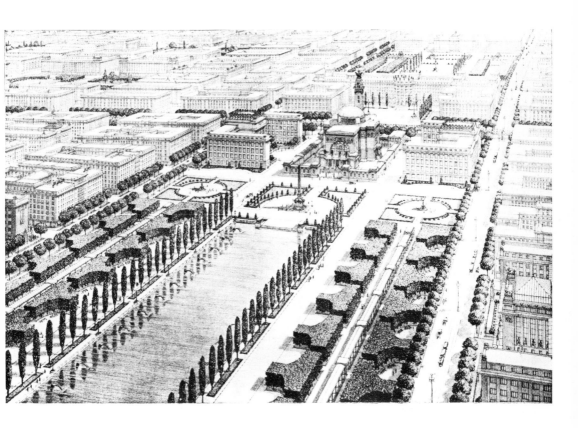

80. Leon Jaussely: urban project for Barcelona, 1903.

81. Cité Industrielle, schematic plan.

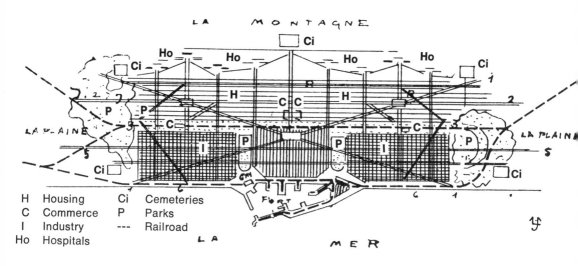

H Housing   Ci Cemeteries
C Commerce P   Parks
I   Industry   --- Railroad
Ho Hospitals

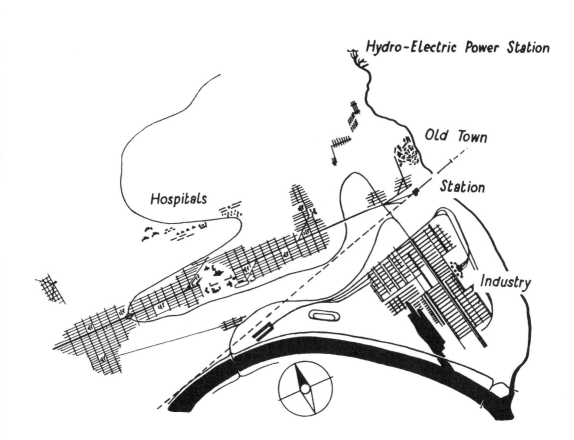

nature, parallels the theories developed by Wagner. Both men seem to have been affected by the common media of an academy and the liberal elements within it. In the case of Wagner, Karl Friedrich von Schinkel's doctrines were the background, and in the case of Garnier, the theories of Henri Labrouste.

Developments in America also seem close to the work of Garnier. The classical revival in American planning coincided with the growth of interest by American architects in education at the École des Beaux-Arts. The Columbian Exposition of 1893, originally planned by Daniel Hudson Burnham (1846–1912), John Wellborn Root (1850–1891), and Frederick Law Olmsted (1822–1903), was a product of this interest (*Fig. 79*).[67] In spite of the pronounced classical vocabulary, remarkably different in spirit from Garnier's approach, the offical buildings of the Exposition were planned as a homogeneous unit of like materials, colors, and cornice heights, similar to the unity of material and style of the Cité. Furthermore, a major consideration was given to the incorporation of nature within the plan: there were approaches to the Exposition by water as well as by land, and a lagoon within a secluded area was an important feature of the plan.[68]

Although this planning of the 1890's was basically formal, the resurgence of the academic tradition did not exclude the creation of an ideal and romantic environment. It can be seen in the natural and sylvan aspects of the Lagoon that formed part of Olmsted's landscaping of the Columbian Exposition, and, to a less obvious degree, in the central municipal area of Wagner's scheme, which was conceived as a park containing a large rectangular pool bordered by poplars and covered walkways. The use of the reflective qualities of water and the shimmering white of the buildings in both these schemes, as well as the importance of landscape as a setting for the architectural monuments, marks a style which has been characterized as an "Arcadian Revival."[69] This title suggests a return directly to antique, and thus pagan, forms, and a growing interest in the spirit behind the architecture of the past; it also involves the concept of beauty as a function meaningful in society. As a description of the spirit of the time, "Arcadian Revival" is also a particularly appropriate term for Garnier's style: his Cité Industrielle is a monumentally conceived and well coordinated plan placed in a parklike setting, where both the classical spirit of the academic tradition and the primitive simplicity of utopian ideals are demonstrated.

CONCLUSION:
RELATION OF THE CITÉ
INDUSTRIELLE TO LATER PLANNING

The Cité Industrielle contains some elements, such as the separation of functions, the consideration of circulation, and the emphasis on industry, that were clearly to become features of modern urban planning. But the direct relationship of the Cité to later developments is less clear. To be sure, the Cité was not altogether unknown: elements of the plan and architecture, along with some theoretical material, were exhibited by Garnier during the 1900's. For example, his residences were seen in 1908,[70] his abattoirs in 1907;[71] his *concours* entries of 1905–1906 for a workers' apartment house project and a bourse can be considered as a continuation of his Cité studies, and as a direct influence on a project for low-cost housing exhibited in 1909.[72] On the other hand, the plan's relative obscurity before its publication in 1917 makes it doubtful that it can be considered as more than an isolated, but possibly the earliest, scheme to take account of and propose solutions to many of the problems which are now associated with twentieth-century planning.

Pawlowski has suggested that the Cité Industrielle influenced Jaussely's project for Barcelona, the Soviet *villes vertes*, the suburbs of Amsterdam, and the Swedish city of Kvarnholmen.[73] Of these, probably only Jaussely's scheme is close enough to that of the Cité (*cf. Figs. 80 and 81*) to be certainly linked with it. The most important connection of Garnier with later planners appears to have been through Le Corbusier, who visited Garnier as early as 1907 and was the first well-known architect publicly to recognize and discuss the Cité Industrielle (1921).[74] It is probably this recognition and, through Le Corbusier, the later writings of critics—especially Sigfried Giedion—that created the role of Garnier as a pioneer of modern architecture and urban planning, and made mention of his name and work mandatory in most later studies of the history of modern architecture and planning. But later interpretations of Garnier and the Cité give only a partial and often distorted picture of the architect's work. Even Le Corbusier's theories on city planning that have a relation to the Cité seem to be developed from the whole complex of ideas originating in the period around the turn of the century, rather than simply from the example of Garnier. And Le Corbusier's conception of the city being transformed into a technical machine differs totally from Garnier's desire to emancipate the inhabitants of the city by means of the machine.[75]

For these reasons it seems that the entire question of Garnier's contribution to twentieth-century architecture and planning—a matter beyond the scope of this study—should be reexamined. Here it is attempted to do no more than present the complex background from which Garnier's plan emerged. This study of the Cité Industrielle as an expression of its environment can only lead to the conclusion that the Cité, one of the most comprehensive ideal plans of any period, and one that was fully related to its contemporary environment, is, probably just because of its comprehensive summation of this environment, an outstandingly original contribution to architectural and planning history.

NOTES

1. Mr. Julien Clarence Levy, who helped Garnier while he was at the Villa Medici with the presentation of this first *envoi*, recalls that Garnier had worked on many large drawings.

   In the anonymous article "Les envois de Rome" (*Construction lyonnaise*, XXIII, July 16, 1901, 164) are mentioned (along with a quotation of Garnier's statement appended to this *envoi*) factories, administration buildings, and workers' housing; it reads, "...M. Tony Garnier has been entirely eliminated [from the exhibition of student work]. He has sent an industrial city, complete factories, administration buildings, workers' housing, and included the following subversive statement: Since all architects rely on false principles, antique architecture is in error. Truth alone is beautiful. In architecture, truth is the result of calculations that are made to satisfy needs by known methods...".

   Finally, it should be noted that the elevation in Garnier's plate includes the dates "1899–1900–1901," possibly referring to the dates during which Garnier was working out the design of the scheme.

2. A barracks has also been considered another essential element that is missing. The most recent comments on this omission have been made by Christophe Pawlowski, *Tony Garnier* (Paris, 1967), pp. 78–79.

3. On the possibility of most of the work being done by 1904, see note 1 above.

4. These renderings are on deposit at the Musée des Beaux-Arts in Lyons.

5. Reproduced in Charles Latham, *The Gardens of Italy* (London, 1905), I, p. 72, fig. 35.

6. Pawlowski, *op. cit.*, pp. 99–113, 150–159.

7. Described by Pawlowski, *op. cit.*, pp. 116–132. The *concours* are cited in the Chronology (pp. 114–115).

8. Pawlowski, *op. cit.*, pp. 26–28.

9. For the development of the automobile industry in Lyons, see Michel Laferrère, *Lyon ville industrielle* (Paris, 1960), pp. 304–305, 362–365.

10. This suggestion is made by Pawlowski, *op. cit.*, p. 79. See Appendix I, pp. 114–115, for the relation made between the Cité and the four existing Rhône cities.

11. Elysée Reclus, "The Evolution of Cities," *Contemporary Review*, LXVII (February, 1895), 246–264.

12. George R. Collins and Christiane Crasemann Collins, "The State of City Planning in Germany and Austria," *Camillo Sitte and the Birth of Modern City Planning* (New York, 1965), pp. 16–25; 118–119, notes 30, 31.

13. Thomas Coglan Horsfall, *The Improvement of the Dwellings and Surroundings of the Peoples: The Example of Germany* (Manchester, 1904), p. 132.

14. Albert Shaw, *Municipal Government in Continental Europe* (New York, 1895), p. 303.

15. *Ibid.*, p. 375.

16. Raymond Unwin, in *Town Planning in Practice* (London, 1909), p. 3, claimed that Horsfall was responsible for the English emulation of German planning. For more on this subject, see also Josephine P. Reynolds, "Thomas Coglan Horsfall and the Town Planning Movement in England," *Town Planning Review*, XXIII (April, 1952), 52–60.

17. See, for instance, Jean Fugaron, "Une manière de l'hygiène," *Le moniteur des architectes*, XXXIX (February, 1890), 9–12; J. Suffit, "Hygiène de la habitation," *L'Architecture*, II (January 12, 1889), 15–16; and "La salubrité," *Le moniteur des architectes*, XLIX (July, 1900), 54–55.

18. See, for instance, "Tribute to the Greatest of Modern Town Planners," *Architectural Review*, XCIII (April, 1943), 90.

19. For these points of view see notes 11 and 14 above.

20. Lewis Mumford, "The Theory and Practice of Regionalism," *Sociological Review*, XX (January, 1928), 30.

21. See, for example, note 18 above.

22. Charles Brun, *Le regionalisme* (Paris, 1911), p. 39. Lewis Mumford, in "The Theory and Practice of Regionalism," p. 317, noted that France was the first country to develop conscious cultural regionalism. Source material can be found in Frédéric Mistral, *Et nous verrons Berre: Pages de doctrine et de critique Félibréene* (Aix en Provence, 1928).

23. Pawlowski, *op. cit.*, p. 24.

24. Garnier had already sent his first study of the Cité Industrielle to Paris when Zola's *Travail* was published in 1901, but he recognized the affinity of his work to Zola's, according to Pierre Bourdeix, "La Cité Industrielle de Tony Garnier," *La construction moderne*, XLI (January 10, 1926), 171, and Gabriel Henriot, "Tony Garnier," *Jardins et Cottages* (October, 1926), p. 14.

25. Bernard Champigneulle, "Tony Garnier, le premier architecte qui a conçu la Cité Industrielle," *Le Figaro littéraire* (February 23, 1948), p. 5.

26. For instance, Zola's *Travail* and Émile Thirion's *Neustria: Utopie individualiste* (Paris, 1901). The utopian schemes may have had English sources. For example, Benjamin Ward Richardson's *Hygeia*, published in 1876, contains a physical description of the city which is similar to that described by Garnier: Richardson's ideas were taken up by Jules Verne in *Les cinq cents millions de la Begum*, published in 1879. Prof. George Collins has called my attention to this similarity.

27. Sigfried Giedion, in *Space, Time and Architecture* (Cambridge, Mass., 1944 [5th ed.], p. 513, note 11, implies that Garnier's emphasis on sports was "progressive" for its period. At the same time that the Cité Industrielle was conceived, Patrick Geddes, in "The Closing Exhibition—Paris 1900," *Contemporary Review*, LXXVIII (November, 1900), 665, spoke of the "revival" of the Olympian games in Athens and Paris.

28. Mentioned in *La Construction moderne*, XIV (July 22, 1899), 509, where this treatment was considered advantageous to eliminate dust and to make cleaning easier.

29. The training and scholarship in Lyons is mentioned in Henri Soilu, "M. Tony Garnier: Grand Prix de Rome pour l'Architecture," *Construction lyonnaise*, XXI (September 16, 1899), 209, and also in Pawlowski, *op. cit.*, p. 32.

30. The Dépôt des Postes et Télégraphes is illustrated in Louis Hautecoeur, *L'Histoire de l'architecture classique*, VII: *La fin de l'architecture classique, 1848–1900* (Paris, 1957), p. 112, fig. 82.

31. For a translation of this document, see note 1 above.

32. Reyner Banham, *Theory and Design in the First Machine Age* (London, 1960), pp. 14–21, and Pawlowski, *op. cit.*, pp. 33–34.

33. Julien Guadet, *Eléments et théorie de l'architecture…* (Paris, 1902), 4 vols.

34. *Ibid.*, II, Book IX, pp. 500–559. However, interest in the pavilion plan seems to

have extended beyond the limits of Guadet's classroom: for examples illustrating its popularity see *La Construction moderne*, III (July 14, 1888) and VI (April 11, 1891), 320ff.

35. For descriptions of the École des Beaux-Arts during this period by American architects who attended this school in the nineties, Eugene Muntz, Walter Cook, Thomas Hastings, John Mead Howells, see *Architectural Record*, X (January, 1901), "The Beaux-Arts Number."

36. A. Ferran, *Philosophie de la composition architecturale* (Paris, 1955), pp. 49–50.

37. Published in *Les concours Edmond Labarre 1881 à 1906...* (Paris, 1907).

38. Dora Wiebenson, "Utopian Aspects of Tony Garnier's Cité Industrielle," *Journal of the Society of Architectural Historians*, XIX (March, 1960), 20, and Pawlowski, *op. cit.*, p. 38.

39. See *Les médailles des concours d'architecture de l'École Nationale des Beaux-Arts de Paris* (Paris, 1890), 15 vols., I: 1898–1899, "Gare centrale de voyageurs pour une capitale."

40. *Les concours Chenavard (section d'architecture)... 1894 à 1907* (Paris, 1907), plates 14–17. Pawlowski, *op. cit.*, p. 46, is the first to have called attention to this project.

41. See *La Construction moderne*, XV (July 7, 1900), 474.

42. Jean Hulot's work, completed in collaboration with Gustav Fougères, was published in 1910.

43. Discussed by Pawlowski, *op. cit.*, pp. 59–66, who claims that this was the first urban project to be selected by a *pensionnaire* at the French Academy in Rome.

44. *Ibid.*, p. 59.

45. Victor Laloux and Paul Monceaux, *Restauration d'Olympie* (Paris, 1889); Alphonse Defrasse and Henri Lechut, *Epidaure* (Paris, 1895); Emmanuel Pontremoli and Maxime Collignon, *Pergame* (Paris, 1900). All these works were begun as fourth-year projects at the Villa Medici. Others that were sent back as fourth-year *envois*, such as Redon's "considerable work" on Baalbek (*La Construction moderne*, V [November 2, 1889], 39), did not achieve publication.

46. Dr. Norman Neuerberg has called my attention to the close relation of Garnier's dam to the cisterns at Villa le Vignacce (see *Fig. 76*), Sette Bassi, Hadrian's Villa in Palestrina, and Cecchignola, as well as to substructures of such buildings as the Villa le Cappellette, the Temple of Claudius in Rome, and especially the ruins of the villa known as Muro Torto, near the French Academy at the Villa Medici. In these examples reverse niches were used as reinforcement against the elements in a manner similar to the operation of the niches in Garnier's dam.

47. For a description of this method, see "The Coignet Reinforced Concrete System," *American Architect and Building News*, XC (September 29, 1906), 101–102.

48. See, for instance, A. L. Cordeau, "Les ciments armés," *Le moniteur des architectes*, XLVII (May, 1899), 25–26; (June, 1899), 44–46; (July, 1899), 52–55; (September, 1899), 69–71; (October, 1899), 75–77.

49. Anatole de Baudot, *L'Architecture: le passé... le présent* (Paris, 1916), pp. 167–168.

50. Such a relationship is made in *American Architect and Building News*, LXXVII (November 29, 1902), 67.

51. See note 28.

52. Pierre Bourdeix, "Tony Garnier précurseur de l'architecture d'aujourd'hui," *L'Architecture d'aujourd'hui* (March, 1931), no. 4, pp. 33ff. Tony Garnier is here quoted as saying at an unspecified date: "In all recognized architecture the style contains ornament, which is only a fashion and does not answer any need. Ornament has, however, reigned in each period. If architecture is to be truthful, it ought to need no ornament, but to exist in its own right."

53. *La Construction moderne*, XIV (July 22, 1899), 509: "This material [concrete]...has the advantage of being plastic. That is, it can be given the most varied forms, and rooms with curved shapes can be designed with this material..."

54. Peter Collins, *Concrete: The Vision of a New Architecture* (London, 1959), pp. 64–75, and L. Mensch, "The Hennebique System," *American Architect and Building News* (November 29, 1902), pp. 67–70; (December 6, 1902), pp. 75–77.

55. Published in *L'Architecture*, XII (October 14, 1899), 383–397.

56. The automobile club terrace was well known. It was also published in *Construction lyonnaise*, XXI (November 1, 1899), 244–246: Carnutensis, "Les jardins sur les toits."

57. Pawlowski, *op. cit.*, p. 28.

58. Several critics have doubted this early date, and have suggested that they were designed around 1917, a date when they would seem to be less "progressive." See Arnold Whittick, *European Architecture in the Twentieth Century* (London, 1950), I, 87–88; and Wiebenson, *op. cit.*, p. 16.

59. "Exposition de Lille," *Le Béton armé* (October, 1902), plate I.

60. It was constructed by M. Dontant for the Champ de Dieppe, out of "a masonry of cut stone, brick, permanent wood forms with cement between the forms, the masonry bedded with a mortar of hydraulic lime," according to "Tribunes de courses," *La Construction moderne*, III (June 4, 1894), 424.

61. Kenneth W. Luckhurst, *The Story of Exhibitions* (London, 1951), p. 182, describes this exhibition as exerting an influence on later electrical developments. He also mentions an even earlier exhibition of the applications of electricity at Paris in 1876.

62. "La construction à Geneve," *La Construction moderne*, XI (October 26, 1895), 42; (November 2, 1895), 56–57; (November 9, 1895), 62–64.

63. Camillo Sitte, *Der Städte-Bau nach seine künstlerischen Grundsätzen* (Vienna, 1889). English edition, *City Building According to Artistic Principles* (New York, 1965).

64. Pierre Lavedan, "L'influence de Haussmann, l'Haussmanisation," *Urbanisme et habitation* (July–December, 1953), pp. 302–305.

65. Otto Wagner, *Die Groszstadt, eine Studie über diese* (Vienna [1911?]).

66. For Wagner's theories see Heinz Geretsegger and Max Peintner, *Otto Wagner: 1841–1918* (Salzburg, 1964), pp. 40–48; and also the abridged translation of Otto Wagner's "Modern Architecture" in *The Brick Builder* (June, 1901), pp. 124–128; (July, 1901), pp. 143–147; (August, 1901), pp. 165–171.

67. Charles Moore, "The World's Columbian Exposition: 1891–1893," *Daniel Burnham, Architect and Planner of Cities* (Boston, 1921), pp. 31–52.

68. These elements were similar to those of the setting of the French Exposition in 1889, to which representatives of the Columbian Exposition had been sent prior to the planning of the American counterpart.

69. The term was used by Christopher Tunnard, *The City of Man* (New York, 1953), p. 308.

70. F. François in "Le salon de la Société lyonnaise des Beaux-Arts," *Construction lyonnaise*, XXXI (April 1, 1908), 76, reports on an exhibition including Garnier's residences held in that year.

71. Garnier's plans for the abattoir were exhibited in the Exposition of Hygiene at Lyons, May, 1907. The Herriot report of the July 28, 1907, *Bulletin municipal officiel*, noted in *Construction lyonnaise*, XXIX (September 16, 1907), 212, but not seen by this author, may contain a detailed description of the project.

72. F. François, in "Le salon de la Société lyonnaise des Beaux-Arts," *Construction lyonnaise*, XXXI (March, 16, 1909), 66, mentions the influence of Garnier's Rotschild project and resultant theories on a project of M. Schaeffer for "Habitations à bon marché."

73. Pawlowski, *op. cit.*, p. 221. However, Pawlowski does not mention his sources or give other evidence for this assumed influence.

74. Le Corbusier, "Trois rappels à messieurs les architectes. III: Le plan," *Esprit Nouveau* (1921), p. 463. Le Corbusier noted in his *Oeuvres complètes, 1910– 1929* (Zurich, 1964), p. 9, that he met Garnier in 1907.

75. It has been suggested that the urban theories connected with Sitte and concerned with a concept of the city as a work of art containing variety and interest, may have been more responsible for the aesthetics of Le Corbusier's planning than were the theories of Garnier: see, for instance, Rudolf Wittkower, "Camillo Sitte's *Art of Building Cities* in an American Translation," *Town Planning Review*, XIX (1947), 164–169.

APPENDIX I

TONY GARNIER'S PREFACE TO
*UNE CITÉ INDUSTRIELLE**

DISPOSITION

The architectural studies presented here with their many illustrations are concerned with the establishment of a new city, Cité Industrielle. Most new towns to be developed will owe their foundation to industrial conditions and the most general case has been considered here. In a city of this kind there normally occur all types of architecture, and it is possible to examine all of them here. In giving the town a medium size (it is assumed to have 35,000 inhabitants), we also pursue the objective of devotion to research of a general nature, which would not be possible in the study of a village or of a very large city. Finally, in this same spirit the site of the city has been chosen so that it contains both mountains and a plain through which a river runs.

The city is imaginary: let us assume that the towns of Rive-de-Gier, Saint-Étienne, Saint Chaumond, Chasse, and Givors have conditions similar to those of this town. The site of this study is located in a region of southeast France, and regional materials have been used in its construction.

Determining factors in the establishment of a similar city should be the proximity of raw materials, or the existence of a natural force capable of being used for energy, or the convenience of methods of transportation. In our case the determining factor in the location of the city is the force of the tributary river that is the power source; there are also mines in the region, but they could be located farther away.

The tributary is dammed; a hydroelectric plant distributes power, light, and heat to the factories and to the entire city.

The principal factories are situated in the plain at the confluence of the river and its tributary. A main-line railroad passes between the factories and the town, which is located above the factories on a plateau. Higher still are placed the hospitals; they, as well as the city, are sheltered from cold winds, and have their terraces oriented to the south. Each of these main elements (factories, town, hospitals) is isolated so that it can expand; allowance has been made for this growth although the study has been pursued from a more general point of view.

Investigation of the most satisfactory program for the material and moral needs of the individual has resulted in the creation of rules concerning road use, hygiene, and so on; the assumption is that a certain progress of social order resulting in an automatic adoption of these rules already has been realized, so that it will not be necessary to enact actual laws. Distribution of land, everything related to the distribution of water, bread, meat, milk, and medical supplies, as well as the re-utilization of refuse, will be given over to the public domain.

*Translation by the present author. The figure numbers have been added to assist the reader.

HABITATIONS

Many towns have already put into effect hygienic rules, which vary according to climatic or geographical conditions. In this city we have imagined that orientation and the general direction of the winds suggest particular architectural practices, of which the following is a summary;

1. In residences, each bedroom ought to have at least one window, large enough to illuminate the whole room and to allow the direct rays of the sun to enter;
2. Courts and light wells, or enclosed spaces used for illumination or ventilation, are prohibited. All spaces, however small, should be lighted and ventilated from the exterior;
3. On the interior of the residences the walls, floors, etc. are to be of smooth materials, with rounded corners.

These rules, required for residences, are also to be applied where possible to the designs of public buildings.

The area of the residential quarter is divided into blocks of 150 meters in the east-west direction and 30 meters in the north-south direction; these blocks are then divided into lots of 15 by 15 meters, one side always abutting on a street [*Figs. 34, 36, 38*]. Such a division provides for the best utilization of the land and satisfies the rules stated above. A residence or any other building may occupy one or more lots, but the building ought always to occupy less than half the total area. The rest of the lot forms a public garden for pedestrian use: that is, on the open part of the lot a public passage should be provided going from the street to the building located behind. This arrangement allows pedestrian circulation through the city in any direction, independent of the street pattern: the land of the town, considered as a whole, is similar to that of a great park, without any wall or enclosure limiting the terrain. The minimum distance between two dwellings in the north-south direction is equal to at least the height of the building situated on the other side. Because of these rules, which do not permit the use of more than half the land and which prohibit enclosures, and also because the land is graded for drainage, there will be variation in the overall design.

The city is composed of a grid of parallel and perpendicular streets. The most important street originates at the station, and runs from east to west. The north-south streets are 20 meters wide and are planted on both sides; the east-west streets are 13 meters or 19 meters wide; those of 19 meters are planted only on the south side, those of 13 meters not planted at all.

ADMINISTRATION—PUBLIC BUILDINGS

In the center of the city a large space is reserved for public buildings [*Figs. 3, 6, 7*]. They form three groups:

I.   Administrative services and assembly rooms.
II. Collections.
III. Facilities for sports and spectacles.

Groups II and III are in a park which is bounded on the north side by

108

the principal street and Group I; on the south a planted terrace opens onto a view of the plain, the river, and the mountains on the other bank.

Group I. The assembly rooms [*Fig. 10*] include:
1. An open-air assembly center for 3,000 people, to be used for meetings and for listening to gramophone recordings of music and parliamentary meetings: for large meetings there will also be;
2. An amphitheater for 1,000 spectators, and two other amphitheaters of 500 seats each. These three rooms are devoted to conferences and projections, etc.
3. A large number of small meeting rooms (each having an office and vestibule) for societies, syndicates, and various other groups.

All these rooms are accessible from a vast portico [*Fig. 13*] forming a covered promenade which is located at the center of the city, and under which a great crowd is able to walk, sheltered from intemperate weather.

To the south of this portico a clock tower [*Fig. 16*], visible for the entire length of the principal street, marks the center of the city from a distance.

The administrative services include:
1. A building containing the offices of the city council, those of the public records (births, marriages, deaths), and those of the tribunal of arbitration, each of these services having public rooms, committee rooms, and office dependencies;
2. Another building composed of offices where all the organs of the city have at least one employee in contact with the administration;
3. A third building for laboratory analysis;
4. Finally, a building, near the firehouse, for the administration archives.

There are also services for labor organizations, which include employment offices, information offices, a group of offices for the syndicates and associations, and hostels and dining halls for accommodating the temporarily unemployed.

There are also medical services, which include a building for medical consultation, a pharmacy for the distribution of medicine, and a hydrotherapeutic medical service.

To the south and on the principal street is the postal service: mail, telegraph, telephone.

Group II. This group includes the following collections:
1. Historical collections, documents important to the city for archaeological, artistic, industrial, or commercial reasons. In the park, outside the rooms containing the collections, are permanent monuments.
2. Botanical collections, in the garden and in a large greenhouse.
3. The library, including a very large reading room, one side of which is reserved for the consulting of works from the library, the other for the periodical and print rooms, and a very large map room in the middle of which is a study map of the world with a raised surface. At the entrance to the library are the indispensable dependencies for cataloguing, bookbinding, classifying, printing, offices for circulating books, etc., and all around, storage space.

4. A large isolated room, with four entrances, designed for temporary exhibitions, where it is possible to present either several simultaneous exhibitions or a single one of greater importance [*Figs. 23–24*].

Group III. Facilities for sports and spectacles include:
1. A room for spectacles and theatrical productions (1,900 seats) [*Fig. 18*], with all the necessary dependencies; a movable stage permitting the reduction of the entr'actes and the suppression of off-stage and above-stage scenery; facilities for the actors, the orchestra, and the scenery; vestibules and toilets, foyer and buffet for the public.
2. A sunken semicircular space, analogous to antique amphitheaters, for outdoor productions, framed by a curtain of trees.
3. Gymnasiums.
4. A large public bath establishment [*Figs. 19–20*], with hot and cold pools, many dressing rooms and baths, shower rooms, massage and resting rooms, a restaurant, a fencing room, and an indoor training track.
5. Area for games (tennis, football, etc.), for training tracks for cyclists and walkers [*Fig. 25*], and for jumping, discus-throwing; etc. Covered tribunals and tiered terraces that are sheltered by trees border one side of these terrains.

Groups II and III are arranged, as has been previously mentioned, in planted gardens, and consequently are traversed by promenades with benches for resting, fountains, etc.

The construction of all the public buildings is of reinforced concrete and reinforced glass.

SCHOOLS

In some parts of the city, chosen for convenience and allocated by district, are located the primary schools for children up to fourteen years [*Fig. 40*]: coeducational schools, that is, the same classes contain boys and girls, the separation of children depending only on their age and advancement in instruction.

A special street landscaped as a garden separates the classes of the younger and older children, and serves as a playground for them while they are waiting for classes; there are also covered and open play yards. Besides classrooms, each school contains a projection room. Nearby are the directors' and superintendents' houses.

At the northeast extremity of the city are the secondary schools; the education given in them is designed for the needs of an industrial city; there is specialized education for a small number of students undertaking administrative or commercial careers, a professional artistic education for a few, and, for the majority, vocational industrial education. These secondary schools are attended by all young people from the age of fourteen to twenty. Some who have been recognized as gifted are directed toward higher education at a special school or college elsewhere.

The professional arts school [*Figs. 28, 30*] is designed to produce craftsmen in the industrial arts who specialize in architecture, painting, sculpture, and all their practical applications in furniture, fabrics, linen, embroidery, costume designing, ceramics, copper, tin or iron work, glasswork, pottery, enamels, printing, lithography, photography, engraving, mosaics, sign-painting, poster-painting, and so on.

The industrial school is concerned mainly with the two principal regional industries, the metallurgic industry and the fabrication of silk. In consequence, a special facility is included whereby all phases of the industrial processing in each of these industries can be followed.

HOSPITALS

The Hospitals (715 beds) [*Figs. 68–70*], situated on the side of the mountain to the north of the center of the city, are sheltered from cold winds by the mountain; curtains of greenery frame them to the east and the west. They contain four principal parts;

    1. The main Hospital Building;
    2. The Heliotherapeutic Building [*Figs. 73–74*];
    3. The Hospital for Contagious Diseases;
    4. The Hospital for Invalids.

The whole and all details are designed according to the latest advancements in medical science. The disposition of each of these elements is arranged so that its expansion is possible.

STATION

The station quarter [*Figs. 53–54*] is zoned mainly for apartment houses [*Figs. 47–51*]: hotels, department stores, etc., so that the rest of the city will be free of high structures. On the plaza facing the station are the open-air markets.

The station [*Fig. 55*], of average size, is at the junction of the great artery coming from the city with the roads that lead to the old city situated beside the mountain tributary; the principal factory operates nearby. The public services of the station are at street level; the tracks below are accessible from platforms and waiting rooms at the lower level. Its large clock tower [*Fig. 55*] is visible throughout the entire city. The freight station is to the east; that of the factory, to the west.

The tracks should be completely straight, so that the trains can move as rapidly as possible.

PUBLIC SERVICES

Certain services are under the jurisdiction of the city administration and are liable to its special dispositions. These services are slaughtering, the manufacture of flour and bread, water service, processing of pharmaceutical products, and dairy products.

The city administration is concerned with the drainage of water and disposal of waste material, with the utilization of refuse; it should also regulate the dam, furnish motor power, light, and heat to the factories and to special areas. It is necessary to have a general installation for

111

this purpose; each locality should be ventilated, heated, illuminated, and should be supplied with hot and cold water, street-cleaning facilities, etc.

FACTORIES

The principal factory [*Fig. 62*] is for metallurgy. Mines in the vicinity produce the raw materials, and steam power is generated from the tributary river facilities.

The factory manufactures pipes and iron bars, extruded iron sections, tools, wheels, machine tools, and agricultural machines; metal frame mountings, the material for railroads and navigation, automobiles and airplanes are made here.

Consequently, it contains blast furnaces, steel-works, space for the large presses and the great hammers, workrooms for mounting and adjusting items, a shipyard for the launching and repairing of boats; a special harbor branching off from the main river, a dock, assembly plants for body work, plants for refractory products, and so on; testing tracks for the different automobiles, numerous laboratories, housing for the engineering personnel. Naturally there are dependencies distributed throughout all sections: toilets, cloakrooms, dining halls, medical aid stations, etc.

Some large avenues, planted quincuncially with trees, connect the different parts of the factory. Each section is arranged in such a manner that it is able to grow independently and without harming the other sections.

On the periphery of these main parts of the city are subsidiary elements: farms for agricultural exploitation, cocooneries, silk-mills, and so on.

CONSTRUCTION

The materials used are concrete for the foundations and walls, and reinforced concrete for the floors and ceilings. All the important buildings are constructed of reinforced concrete.

These two materials are prepared in molds made for this purpose. The simpler the molds, the easier will be the construction, and consequently the less the cost. This simplicity of means leads logically to a great simplicity of expression in the structure. Let us note also that, if our structure remains simple, unadorned, without molding, bare, we are then best able to arrange the decorative arts so that each object of art will retain its purest and clearest expression because it will be totally independent of the construction. Besides, who would not see that the use of such materials results in the obtaining of the horizontals and verticals that are proper to give to the construction that calm and equilibrium that will harmonize with the lines of nature? Other systems of construction, other materials, lead, without doubt, to other forms which it would also be interesting to study.

Here is summarized the program of the planning of a city, in which it is exemplified that work is the human law and that there is enough of the ideal in the cult of beauty and order to endow life with splendor.

APPENDIX II

CONTENTS OF
UNE CITÉ INDUSTRIELLE

CHRONOLOGY

1869   Tony Garnier born at Lyons

1886–1889   Studied at École des Beaux-Arts, Lyons

1889–1899   Studied at École des Beaux Arts, Paris

1899–1904   *Prix de Rome* student at French Academy in Villa Medici, Rome

Work completed by Garnier before publication of *Une Cité Industrielle*.

1905   Dairy, Lyons

1905   Rotschild competition for a low-cost workers' housing project, Paris

1906   Competition for a bourse, Marseilles

1907   Competition for an abattoir and market, Reims

1908–1924   Abattoirs de La Mouche, Lyons

1909–1911   Three villas near Lyons

1911–1927   Hospital of the Grange-Blanche, Lyons

1913–1918   Municipal Stadium, Lyons

1913–1914   Chief architect for International Urban Exposition, Lyons

Publications

Tusculum, état actuel et restauration (Paris, n.d.).

Une cité industrielle, étude pour la construction des villes (Paris, 1917). Second edition, 1932.

Les grands travaux de la ville de Lyon (Paris, n.d.).
   Hospital of the Grange-Blanche
   Stadium
   School for applied arts
   Dairy
   Project for a pasteurization plant
   Project for a bourse
   Textile school
   Multiple-dwelling units
   Stockyard and abattoirs
   Project for a central postal, telegraph, and telephone service
   Vaudrey telephone office
   Monument aux Morts
   Designs for individual monuments

Work completed by Garnier after publication of *Une Cité Industrielle*

1920–1935	Living quarters of the États-Unis, Lyons
1924	Monument to the Dead, Lyons
1925	Pavilion of Lyon-Saint-Étienne, Paris, Exposition des arts décoratifs
1927	Telephone office, Lyons
1929	Project for a monument to Christopher Columbus, Santo-Domingo
1930–1933	Textile school, Lyons
1931–1934	Town hall, Boulogne-Billancourt
1935–1939	Competition for theater, Saint-Étienne
	Competition for hospital, Reims
	Competition for park, Lyons
1948	Tony Garnier died at Bedoule

BIBLIOGRAPHY

The arrangement is chronological. A dagger (†) indicates that a reference is cited by Pawlowski but has not been consulted by the present author.

1894–1900

"Concours de Rome," *Construction moderne*, IX (August 11, 1894), 529–531.

"Les grands prix de Rome," *Construction moderne*, X (August 10, 1895), 529–531; (September 7, 1895), 577–580.

Rümler, E. "Le concours du prix de Rome," *Construction moderne*, XI (August 8, 1896), 529–530.

Les Concours Edmond Labarre: 1881 à 1906. Paris, 1907. Plate 17: "Un jardin d'acclimation," 1896.

Les Concours Chenavard (section d'architecture) à l'École Nationale des Beaux-Arts, 1894–1907, Vol. II. Paris, 1907. Plates 91–95: "Un jardin botanique," 1899.

Rivoalen, E. "Le concours du grand prix d'architecture," *Construction moderne*, XII (August 21, 1897), 555–556.

———. "Les grands prix d'architecture en 1898," *Construction moderne*, XIII (August 6, 1898), 529–530.

———. "Le concours du grand prix de Rome en 1899," *Construction moderne*, XIV (August 12, 1899), 541–543; (August 26, 1899), 567–569.

Soilu, H. "M. Tony Garnier: Grand prix de Rome pour l'architecture," *Construction lyonnaise*, XXI (September 16, 1899), 209.

———. "Concours pour le Grand Prix de Rome: Le projet de M. Tony Garnier," *Construction lyonnaise* (October 1, 1899), 222–224.

Les médailles des concours d'architecture de l'École Nationale des Beaux-Arts, I: 1898–1899. Paris. Plates 121, 138, 185, 185 bis, 216–219.

Les grands prix de Rome d'architecture de 1850 à 1900. Paris, n.d. Plates 421–424, 442–445, 457–463.

B. L. "Banquet du Syndicat des Architectes," *Construction lyonnaise*, XXI (December 1, 1899), 269.

"Banquet offert le 2 décembre 1899 aux Prix de Rome: MM. Tony Garnier, architecte, André Vermare, statuaire," *Construction lyonnaise*, XXII (January 1, 1900), 2–3.

1901–1910

"Les envois de Rome en 1901," *L'Architecture*, XIV (July 13, 1901), 242–243.

"Les envois de Rome," *Construction lyonnaise*, XXIII (July 16, 1901), 164.

Malézieux, J. "A. M. Tony Garnier," *Construction lyonnaise* (August 16, 1901), p. 184.

Planat, P. "Envois de Rome," *Construction moderne*, XVII (August 8, 1903), 529–531.

"Les envois de Rome," *Construction moderne*, XIX (July 9, 1904), 482.

"Les envois de Rome," *L'Architecture*, XVII (July 9, 1904), 267.

"L'Exposition des envois de Rome," *Construction lyonnaise*, XXVI (July 16, 1904), 162.

"Le concours Rotschild," *Construction moderne*, XX (April 15, 1905), 339; (July 8, 1905), 483.

"Concours de la Fondation Rotschild," *Les concours publics d'architecture*, IX (1906), 1–8, plates 1–33.

Planat, P. "Le concours de Marseille," *Construction moderne*, XXI (January 27, 1906), 193–196; (February 10, 1906), 223–224, 227–228.

"Vacherie municipale à Lyon," *Construction moderne*, XXI (March 10, 1906), 267–268.

Tuotiop, A. "La vacherie munipale au parc de la Tête d'Or," *Construction lyonnaise*, XXIII (June 1, 1906), 125–128.

"Marseille, rénovation des quartiers situés derrière la Bourse," *Les concours publics d'architecture*, IX (1906), 57–58, plates 99–103.

Soilu, H. "Le salon de la Société lyonnaise des Beaux-Arts: L'architecture," *Construction lyonnaise*, XXIX (March 16, 1907), 62–63.

"A propos du concours de Reims," *Les concours publics d'architecture*, XI (1908), 5–8, plates 9–11.

Françon, F. "Le salon de la Société lyonnaise des Beaux-Arts: L'architecture," *Construction lyonnaise*, XXX (April 1, 1908), 76.

"Les abattoirs de la mouche à Lyon," *Construction lyonnaise*, XXI (January 16, 1909), 16–20.

"Designation de l'Architecte Directeur de Travaux de Construction du futur Hôtel-Dieu de Lyon," *Construction lyonnaise*, XXXI (November 16, 1909), 260.

† Herriot, E. and Tony Garnier. *La désaffection de l' Hôtel-Dieu*. Lyons, 1910.

"Le futur Hôtel-Dieu de Lyon," *Construction lyonnaise*, XXXII (March 16, 1910), 63.

1911–1920

De Souza, R. *Nice: capitale d'hiver*. Paris, 1913, p. 405.

† "Exposition international urbaine à Lyon," *Lyon Exposition*, 1913.

† "Le grand hall de l'exposition dûe à Tony Garnier," *Lyon Exposition*, 1913.

† "L'affiche de l'exposition dûe à Tony Garnier," *Lyon Exposition*, 1913.

"Le nouvel hôpital de Lyon," *Construction lyonnaise*, XXXV (August 16, 1913), 183–188; (September 1, 1913), 198–199.

"Un stade pour la pratique des sports," *Construction lyonnaise*, XXXV (September 16, 1913), 207.

Herriot, E. "L'Architecture," *L'Opinion* (March 9, 1918), p. 205.

1921–1930

Le Corbusier, "Trois rappels à messieurs les architectes. III: Le plan," *Esprit nouveau* (1921), No. 4, p. 463 (reprinted in *Vers une architecture*. Paris, 1923, pp. 38–41).

Doillet, L. "L'Île des morts à Lyon," *L'Architecture*, XXXVI (July 25, 1923), 203–209.

Badovici, J. "Un monument aux morts à Lyon," *L'Architecture vivante*, II (Fall–Winter, 1924), 23.

† Deshairs, L. Preface to *Catalogue d'exposition de Tony Garnier au Musée des Arts Décoratifs à Paris*. Paris, 1925.

Vitry, P. "L'Exposition des arts décoratifs modernes," *Gazette des Beaux-Arts*, LXVII (July, 1925), 1–18.

Bourdeix, P. "A propos de l'exposition de Tony Garnier au Musée des Arts Décoratifs à Paris," *Construction moderne*, XL (April 5, 1925), 313–315.

Brincourt, M. "A propos d'une exposition de dessins de Tony Garnier," *L'Architecture*, XXXVII (May 10, 1925), 137–139.

Papini, R. "Le arti a Parigi nel 1925: l'architettura," *Architettura e arti decorative*, V (1925–1926), 201–233.

Bourdeix, P. "La Cité Industrielle de Tony Garnier," *Construction moderne*, XLI (January 10, 1926), 170–176.

A. G. "A l'exposition des arts décoratifs—le pavillon de Lyon-Saint Étienne," *Construction moderne*, XLI (January 10, 1926), 169–170.

Henriot, G. "Tony Garnier," *Jardins et Cottages* (October, 1926), pp. 1–25.

Dormoy, M. "L'Architecture moderne: Tony Garnier," *L'Art vivante* (December, 1926), pp. 888–889.

Augros, P. *Le Béton armé* (Paris, 1926), pp. 193–194, 200, 242–243, 264.

Deshairs, Léon. "Les dessins de Tony Garnier," *Art et décoration*, L (January–June, 1926), 61–64.

Garnier, Tony. Preface to M. Kharachnick, *Quelques problèmes d'urbanisme*. Paris, 1927.

Robertson, H. "A Hospital in the Making: The Grange Blanche Hospital, Lyon," *Architect and Building News*, CXVIII (July, 1927), 19–23.

————. "The Stadium at Lyon," *Architect and Building News*, CXVIII (July 29, 1927), 197–200.

————. "The Home of a Great French Architect, the Villa of Tony Garnier at Lyon," *Architect and Building News*, CXVIII (October 7, 1927), 577–581.

Dormoy, M. "Tony Garnier," *L'Amour de l'art*, VIII (February, 1927), no. 1, 38–42.

Giedion, Sigfried. *Bauen in Frankreich: Eisen, Eisenbeton*. Leipzig, 1928, pp. 77–83.

"Marché aux bestiaux et abattoirs de la mouche à Lyon," *Cahiers d'art*, III (1928), No. 8, 343–351.

Marconi, P. "Mostra Romana del concorso per il faro alla memoria di Cristoforo Columbiano," *L'Architettura et arti decorative*, IX (September, 1929), 100–135.

Taut, Bruno. "Project for the Quartier des États-Unis," *Modern Architecture*. London, 1929, p. 48.

"Tony Garnier, architecte...," *Institut de France—Académie des Beaux-Arts*, V (January–June, 1929), Bull. 9, pp. 69–70.

Malkiel-Jirmounsky, M. *Les tendances de l'architecture contemporaine*. Paris, 1930, pp. 27–51.

† Malespine, R. *L'Urbanisme nouveau*. Lyons, 1930.

Garnier, Tony. Preface to J. Magnillac, *Barèmes pour le calcul simplifié des charpentes en bois, charpentes en fer et du béton armé*. Lyons, 1930.

1931–1940

Bourdeix, P. "Tony Garnier précurseur de l'architecture d'aujourd'hui," *L'Architecture d'aujourd'hui* (March, 1931), no. 4, pp. 33–38.

Goissaud, A. "Chez l'architecte Tony Garnier—Grand Prix de Rome," *Construction moderne*, XLVIII (November 6, 1932), 82–87.

Badovici, J. "L'Œuvre de Tony Garnier," *L'Architecture vivante*, X (Spring–Summer, 1932).

"Hôtel de Ville de Boulogne-Billancourt (Seine), Tony Garnier et J. Debat-Ponson, architectes," *Architecte*, XI (n.s.) (November, 1934), 121–129.

See, C. E. "Le nouvel hôtel de ville de Boulogne-Billancourt," *Construction moderne*, L (November 4, 1934), 106–128.

Posener, Julius. "La Cité Industrielle de Tony Garnier (introduction à une étude sur l'habitation à bon marché)", *L'Architecture d'aujourd'hui*, VI (5 ser.) (July, 1935), 4–5.

Zahar, M. "La nouvelle mairie de Boulogne-Billancourt," *Art et décoration*, LXIV (January, 1935), 28–33.

Morizet, A. "Hôtel de ville de Boulogne-sur-Seine," *L'Architecture*, XLVII (1935), 159–170.

Pevsner, Nikolaus. *Pioneers of the Modern Movement*. London, 1936, pp. 175–176 (2nd ed., *Pioneers of Modern Design from William Morris to Walter Gropius*. New York, 1949, pp. 110–113).

† *Inauguration du buste de Tony Garnier à l'hôpital E. Herriot le 24 Octobre 1937*, 1937.

† Garnier, Tony. *Rapport général sur l'état des bâtiments départmentaux*. Lyons, 1937.

"Hommage à Tony Garnier," *Construction moderne*, LIII (November 21, 1937), iii–ix.

"Hôpital Edouard Herriot à Lyon (Hôpital de Grange-Blanche)," *Construction moderne*, LII (August 8, 1937), 741–756.

Badovici, J. and A. Morancé, *L' Œuvre de Tony Garnier*. Paris, 1938.

1941–1950

Giedion, Sigfried. *Space, Time and Architecture*. Cambridge. Mass, 1941, pp. 253–255.

"Tribute to the Greatest of Modern Town Planners," *Architectural Review*, XCIII (April, 1943), xxxix, 90.

Bardet, G. *Pierre sur pierre*. Paris, 1945, p. 166.

Le Corbusier, *Manière de penser l'urbanisme*. Paris, 1946, p. 38.

Hermant, A. "Tissus residentiels," *Techniques et architecture* (1947), nos. 7–8, p. 337.

Gille-Delafon, S. "Précurseur de l'architecture d'aujourd'hui: Tony Garnier est mort," *Arts* (February 20, 1948), p. 5.

Champigneulle, B. "Tony Garnier, le premier architecte qui a conçu la Cité Industrielle," *Figaro littéraire* (February 28, 1948), p. 5.

"Una cuidad industrial," *Revista de arquitectura*, XXXIII (November, 1948), 324–343.

Montagne, C. "Tony Garnier de l'Académie de France à Rome, architecte à Lyon," *L'architecture d'aujourd'hui*, XIX (April, 1948), v.

Veronesi, Giulia. *Tony Garnier, 1869–1947*. Milan, 1948.

Soulillou, A. "Tony Garnier est mort, un précurseur de l'architecture sociale," *Chantiers dans le monde* (March–April, 1948), pp. 40–42.

Veronesi, Giulia. "Tony Garnier, l'architetto della prima città industriale," *Emporium*, CVIII (September, 1948), 143–145.

†———. "E' morto un grande architetto," *Il nuovo corriere* (May, 1948).

———. *The Architect's Journal*, CVII (March 11, 1948), 234.

———. *Architectural Review*, CIII (May, 1948), 224.

———. *The Builder*, CXXLIV (April 9, 1948), 435.

———. *Journal of the Royal Institute of British Architects*, LV (3 ser.) (May, 1948), 321.

"A.R.," *Das Werk*, XXXV (July, 1948), 90–91.

Bardet, G. *Le nouvel urbanisme*. Paris, 1948, pp. 26–27, 29.

†"Tony Garnier, grande figure de l'architecture moderne," *Œuvres—Maîtres d'œuvres* (1949), no. 16, pp. 1–18.

Zevi, Bruno. *Storia dell'architettura moderna*. Milan, 1950, pp. 101–105.

Whittick, Arnold. *European Architecture in the Twentieth Century*. Vol. I. London, 1950, pp. 87–88, 115–117.

1951–1960

Tony Garnier: 1869–1948. Lyons, 1951 (preface, E. Herriot; biography, L. Piessat).

†Lerrant, J. J. "Tony Garnier au musée des Beaux-Arts de Lyon," *Bulletin des musées lyonnais*, II (1953), 45–53.

Marrast, J. "Tony Garnier," *L'Architecture française* (June, 1955), no. 155–156, p. 7.

Ferran, A. *Philosophie de la composition architecturale*. Paris, 1955, pp. 49–50.

Ragon, M. *Le livre de l'architecture moderne*. Paris, 1958, pp. 79, 81–82, 142, 294.

Hitchcock, Henry-Russell. *Architecture: Nineteenth and Twentieth Centuries*. London, 1958, pp. 317–319.

Collins, George R. "Linear Planning throughout the World," *Journal of the Society of Architectural Historians*, XVIII (October, 1959), 74–93.

Rosenau, H. *The Ideal City*. London, 1959, pp. 143–144.

† *Les Sources du XXe siècle: Les Arts en Europe de 1884 à 1914* (exhibition catalogue, Musée National d'Art Moderne). Paris, 1960.

Benevolo, L. *Storia dell'architettura moderna*. Vol. I. Bari, 1960, pp. 430–442.

Wiebenson, Dora, "Utopian Aspects of Tony Garnier's Cité Industrielle," *Journal of the Society of Architectural Historians*, XIX (March, 1960), 16–24 (summary in *Ekistics*, September, 1960).

"Linear Planning throughout the World," *Ekistics* (April, 1960).

Banham, Reyner. *Theory and Design in the First Machine Age*. London, 1960, pp. 35–38.

Hautecœur, Louis. "Henri Prost à la Villa Medicis (1902–1907)," *L'Œuvre de Henry Prost*. Paris, 1960, pp. 13–27.

1961–1968

"La mostra dei disegni di Tony Garnier," *L'architettura, cronache e storia*, VII (December, 1961), 569.

† "Une exposition de l'œuvre de Tony Garnier à Rome," *Bulletin de la Société des Architectes Diplomés par le Gouvernement*. 1961, No. 102.

Tintori, S. "Garnier technico e politico della cità industriale," *Casabella continuità* (September, 1961), No. 255, pp. 42–52.

Mumford, Lewis. *The City in History*. London, 1961, p. 596.

Veronesi, Giulia. "Visioni di un architetto poeta: I disegni de Tony Garnier," *Comunita*, XV (May, 1961), No. 89, pp. 93–108.

Michelis, P. A. *Esthétique de l'architecture du béton armé*. Paris, 1963, p. 127.

Morini, M. *Atlante di storia dell'urbanistica*. Milan, 1963, pp. 336–337, 360–361.

Besset, M. "Tony Garnier," *Dictionnaire de l'architecture moderne*. Paris, 1964, pp. 134–135.

Choay, Françoise. *L'Urbanisme, utopies et réalités*. Paris, 1965, pp. 209–219.

Delevoy, Robert. *Dimensions du XXème siècle: 1900–1945*. Geneva, 1965, p. 49.

† Bourdeix, P. *Tony Garnier et son œuvre*. Paris, 1966.

Pawlowski, Christophe. *Tony Garnier et les debuts de l'urbanisme fonctionnel en France*. Paris, 1967.

Wiebenson, Dora. Review of C. Pawlowski, *Tony Garnier...*, *Journal of the Society of Architectural Historians*, XXVII (December, 1968), 304–305.

INDEX

SOURCES OF ILLUSTRATIONS

Architectural Review (April, 1943): 81.

Architecture (October, 1899): 41.

Concours Chenavard II (Paris, 1907): 43.

Concours Edmond Labarre (Paris, 1907): 71.

Construction moderne (June, 1898): 26; (October, 1899): 15.

Courtesy French Government Tourist Office: 56.

Tony Garnier, *Une Cité Industrielle* (Paris, 1932): 2, 3, 4, 6, 7, 8, 10, 13, 16, 18, 19, 20, 21, 23, 24, 25, 28, 30, 32, 33, 34, 35, 36, 37, 38, 39, 40, 42, 44, 47, 48, 49, 50, 51, 53, 54, 55, 59, 60, 62, 65, 67, 68, 69, 70, 73, 74, 77;

Tony Garnier, *Grands travaux de Lyon* (Paris, 1920): 9, 12, 29, 45, 46, 61, 63, 64, 72.

Sigfried Giedion, *Space, Time and Architecture* (Cambridge, Mass.: Harvard University Press, 1941): 11, 66.

Giraudon, Paris: 31.

Charles Latham, *Villas of Italy* (London, 1905): 27.

Le Béton armé (October, 1900): 17, 57; (October, 1902): 58; (January, 1905): 75; (January, 1914): 52.

Memorie della ponti academia romana di archeologia II, 1928: 76.

Charles Moore, *Daniel Burnham* (Boston, 1921): 79.

Emmanuel Pontremoli, *Pergame* (Paris, 1900): 5, 22.

R. de Souza, *Nice: capital d'hiver* (Paris, 1913): 80.

Otto Wagner, *Die Groszstadt...* (Vienna [1911?]): 78.

Arnold Whittick, *European Architecture in the Twentieth Century* (London, 1950): 14.

Dora Wiebenson: 1.